Jonathan Swift's
GULLIVER'S TRAVELS

NOTES

A CONTEMPORARY
LITERARY VIEWS BOOK

Edited and with an Introduction by
HAROLD BLOOM

© 1996 by Chelsea House Publishers, a division of Main Line Book Co.

Introduction © 1996 by Harold Bloom

All rights reserved. No part of this publication may be reproduced or transmitted in any form or by any means without the written permission of the publisher.

Printed and bound in the United States of America.

First Printing
1 3 5 7 9 8 6 4 2

Cover Illustration: The Bettmann Archive

Library of Congress Cataloging-in-Publication Data

Bloom, Harold.
Jonathan Swift's Gulliver's travels / Harold Bloom, editor.
p. cm – (Bloom's notes)
Includes bibliographical references and index.
Summary: Includes a brief biography of Jonathan Swift, thematic and structural analysis of the work, critical views, and an index of themes and ideas.
ISBN 0-7910-3665-0
1. Swift, Jonathan, 1667–1745. Gulliver's travels. 2. Satire, English—History and criticism. 3. Voyages, Imaginary, in literature. [1. Swift, Jonathan, 1667–1745. Gulliver's travels. 2. English literature—History and criticism.] I. Title. II. Series: Bloom, Harold. Bloom's notes.
PR3724.G8B56 1996
823'.5—dc20
95-34515
CIP
AC

Chelsea House Publishers
1974 Sproul Road, Suite 400
P.O. Box 914
Broomall, PA 19008-0914

Contents

User's Guide	4
Introduction	5
Biography of Jonathan Swift	8
Thematic and Structural Analysis	11
List of Characters	24
Critical Views	25
Books by Jonathan Swift	66
Works about Jonathan Swift and *Gulliver's Travels*	70
Index of Themes and Ideas	74

User's Guide

This volume is designed to present biographical, critical, and bibliographical information on Jonathan Swift and *Gulliver's Travels*. Following Harold Bloom's introduction, there appears a detailed biography of the author, discussing the major events in his life and his important literary works. Then follows a thematic and structural analysis of the work, in which significant themes, patterns, and motifs are traced. An annotated list of characters supplies brief information on the chief characters in the work.

A selection of critical extracts, derived from previously published material by leading critics, then follows. The extracts consist of statements by the author on his work, early reviews of the work, and later evaluations down to the present day. The items are arranged chronologically by date of first publication. A bibliography of Swift's writings (including a selected listing of books he wrote, cowrote, edited, and translated in his lifetime, and important posthumous publications), a list of additional books and articles on him and on *Gulliver's Travels,* and an index of themes and ideas conclude the volume.

Harold Bloom is Sterling Professor of the Humanities at Yale University and Henry W. and Albert A. Berg Professor of English at the New York University Graduate School. He is the author of twenty books and the editor of more than thirty anthologies of literature and literary criticism.

Professor Bloom's works include *Shelley's Mythmaking* (1959), *The Visionary Company* (1961), *Blake's Apocalypse* (1963), *Yeats* (1970), *A Map of Misreading* (1975), *Kabbalah and Criticism* (1975), and *Agon: Towards a Theory of Revisionism* (1982). *The Anxiety of Influence* (1973) sets forth Professor Bloom's provocative theory of the literary relationships between the great writers and their predecessors. His most recent books are *The American Religion* (1992) and *The Western Canon* (1994).

Professor Bloom earned his Ph.D. from Yale University in 1955 and has served on the Yale faculty since then. He is a 1985 MacArthur Foundation Award recipient and served as the Charles Eliot Norton Professor of Poetry at Harvard University in 1987–88. He is currently the editor of the Chelsea House series Major Literary Characters and Modern Critical Views, and other Chelsea House series in literary criticism.

Introduction

HAROLD BLOOM

Dr. Samuel Johnson, in my judgment foremost among all literary critics, had a great aversion to *Gulliver's Travels*. This always surprises me, because Johnson greatly appreciated "invention" or literary originality, and Swift's picaresque voyages of Lemuel Gulliver are surpassingly original. But Johnson feared madness, and he sensed elements in the book that did not seem to him fully balanced or wholly sane. There is a fine madness in the Third and Fourth Voyages of *Gulliver's Travels*, though I do not mean to suggest that actual madness on Swift's part was involved. Swift was declared insane in 1742, sixteen years after *Gulliver's Travels* was published, but the book itself, written at the height of his powers, is dangerously sane, and would not hurt so much as it does if it were not informed by a savage lucidity, and by a very severe rationality. The complacent, gullible Gulliver, who is anything but his author's spokesperson, is partly insane as the book ends, because he has trapped himself in the perspective of the rational horses, the Houyhnhnms, and so regards himself, and his long-suffering wife, as abominable Yahoos. Swift, despite his own horror of false human pride, knows the limits both of Gulliver and of the Houyhnhnms, and Swift expects us, his readers, to learn just what those limits are.

Perhaps because it has become a bowdlerized work for children, the First Voyage, to Lilliput, the land of the little people, has remained the most famous, though it lacks the inventiveness of the Third Voyage, particularly to Laputa, the floating island, and the shocking greatness of the Fourth Voyage, to Houyhnhnmland. Yet even the First Voyage exposes Gulliver to us as a good observer incapable of seeing what most matters, wherever he goes. Literal-minded, totally unimaginative, humorless, poor Gulliver invariably adopts for himself the social prejudices and ruling perspectives that dominate each land he visits. Sublimely, he invariably at once sees everything and sees nothing, which is precisely what Swift desires to heal in us. *Gulliver's Travels* is written to cleanse our blindness, to cure us of *our own unconscious ironies.* Martin Price remarks that "Gulliver is invented as the hero of a comedy of incomprehension." Since each of us, to some extent, lives a comedy of incomprehension, we find Gulliver not unsympathetic. Gulliver is Everyman as society's dupe, accepting insane conventions because he cannot see through them or around them.

Swift's modern critics rightly emphasize that Gulliver's essential weakness is his inability to understand the paradox that man is an animal capable of reason, rather than either a rational or irrational beast as such. Gulliver sees only the two extremes, and so is prone to easy judgments and false moral conclusions. At the center of Gulliver's character is a contradictory stance that features both blind pride and self-contempt. This inner confusion leads to Gulliver's torment in the Fourth Voyage, when he sees that he is, compared to the rational horses, only a superior kind of Yahoo, an irrational beast suspiciously resembling man. It is not at all a simple matter to interpret what the Yahoos represent, but we can see readily enough what they are *not.* Neither the Christian nor the Classical view of the human is embodied in the Yahoos; they are natural men as conceived by Swift, who was both Christian and humanist, but above all else an indignant ironist, unable to forgive the folly of human pride and self-love. Since we all of us personally know a number of Yahoos, even if they are better washed than Swift's brutes, we all of us can feel a touch uncomfortable when we confront the Yahoo within each of us. Clearly, Swift intended our discomfort, and we have difficulty in disputing his moral designs upon us, at least in this regard.

Yet the Houyhnhnms present us with a larger problem, whether for interpretation or as moral instruction. They reason more or less splendidly, but they are incapable of impulse and are altogether devoid of imagination. This certainly does not bother Gulliver, yet it should and does bother us. It was, after all, a Yahoo who wrote *Hamlet* and *King Lear,* and another Yahoo who wrote *Gulliver's Travels,* a narrative that no Houyhnhnm could hope to comprehend. Does Swift actually intend us to regard the Houyhnhnms as admirable? Are we or are we not Yahoos, according to Swift? So pervasive and absolute is Swift's irony that these questions may remain forever unanswerable. All that the Houyhnhnms disagree about, among themselves, is the best way to decimate and ultimately exterminate the Yahoos. In the century of the Nazi death camps, the Houyhnhnms are likely to seem rather more sinister to us than Swift, with all his ironies, could have intended. ✣

Biography of Jonathan Swift

Jonathan Swift was born in Dublin on November 30, 1667, seven months after his father's death. He was the son of Jonathan Swift and Abigaile Erick (or Herrick); since both parents were from England, Swift, though born and educated in Ireland, did not think of himself as Irish. He attended Kilkenny Grammar School from around 1673 to 1681, then went to Trinity College, Dublin, where, because of disciplinary problems, he obtained his B.A. degree in 1686 only "by special grace" (*speciali gratia*).

In 1689 Swift left for England, becoming secretary to Sir William Temple, through whom he apparently hoped to achieve some advancement in political affairs. Nothing came of this association, however, and, having received his M.A. degree in 1692 from Hart Hall, Oxford, Swift took orders as a priest of the Anglican Church of Ireland early in 1695, more to achieve independence than out of any particular religious fervor.

After spending an unhappy year as vicar of Kilroot in northern Ireland, Swift returned to England and remained with Temple at Moor Park until 1699. It was during this period that he began his literary career. He had published his first poem, "Ode to the Athenian Society," in 1691; now, in 1696, he wrote *A Tale of a Tub,* which was primarily an attack on various religious abuses. Shortly thereafter he wrote *The Battel of the Books,* a satirical treatment of the disputes between the Ancients (those who, like Sir William Temple, favored the ancient Latin and Greek writers) and the Moderns (those who believed that contemporary writers had equaled or exceeded the ancients in literary merit). The controversy focused around Temple's championing of the *Epistles of Phalaris,* a work he believed to have been written in classical times. Temple was attacked by several of the Moderns, including Richard Bentley (who was, however, a leading classical scholar), who established conclusively that the *Epistles* were spurious. Swift's *Battel* defends Temple by satirizing his opponents.

Temple died in 1699, leaving Swift without a patron. He returned to Ireland, settling this time in Dublin as the chaplain to Lord Berkeley, the new Lord Justice of Ireland. In 1704 Swift published *A Tale of the Tub* (along with *The Battel of the Books*). His outspokenness, which was manifested also in a number of pamphlets on religious questions, such as "An Argument against Abolishing Christianity" (1708), made it harder for Swift to gain the preferment that would have enabled him to leave Ireland. He continued to sharpen his satirical skills, however, by poking fun at an astrologer, John Partrige, writing several pamphlets in 1708 in which he claimed that he had predicted Partrige's death; after this, Partrige had considerable difficulty proving that he was still alive.

Swift was a frequent visitor to England, where he gained a literary reputation, became acquainted with Joseph Addison, Richard Steele, Alexander Pope, and William Congreve, and was briefly, in 1714, a member of the Scriblerus Club with Pope, John Gay, John Arbuthnot, and others. In 1710 he switched his political allegiance to the Tories and was active as a political journalist, writing poems and tracts in support of the Tory ministry and editing *The Examiner* for four years. During this time his relationship with Esther Johnson ("Stella") flourished. He had first met her around 1690, when he was her tutor. Around 1700 she settled near Dublin to be near him. Swift's *Journal to Stella* was written between 1710 and 1713. Some biographers believe that he married her in 1716. Around 1715 a woman named Esther Vanhomrigh fell in love with Swift and followed him to Ireland, but he rejected her. His poem *Cadenus and Vanessa* (1726) deals with this relationship.

In 1713 Swift became Dean of St. Patrick's Cathedral in Dublin, the highest position he was ever to achieve. The death of Queen Anne in 1714 and the subsequent ascendancy of the Whigs put an end to his political career and ensured that he would remain in Ireland for most of the rest of his life, a fate he increasingly resented. He nevertheless wrote several pamphlets in defense of Irish rights, most notably *The Drapier's Letters* (1724–25), which frustrated an attempt to circulate debased currency in Ireland and made him a popular hero.

Swift may have begun working on *Gulliver's Travels* as early as 1720; published in 1726, it satirized contemporary politics and the conventions of both philosophical and "factual" tales of exploration. In that year Swift visited Alexander Pope at his estate in Twickenham, and it was at that time that they planned the series of volumes published in 1727 as *Miscellanies in Prose and Verse;* the first volume (a revision of a book of the same title issued in 1711) was entirely by Swift, and the other two volumes contained work by him as well as by Pope, Arbuthnot, and Gay. Two further volumes appeared in 1732 and 1735. *A Modest Proposal,* a famous satire recommending that the children of poor people should be fattened to feed the rich, was published in 1729, and *Verses on the Death of Dr. Swift,* both a self-parody and an attack on women, appeared in 1731.

Swift had, since his twenty-third year, suffered from a condition now called Meniere's disease, which causes nausea and loss of equilibrium. Late in his life he began to develop a brain tumor; in 1742 he lapsed into dementia, dying on October 19, 1745.

Swift was a tremendously prolific poet, pamphleteer, and essayist, and many editions of his collected works, as well as letters and other unpublished or uncollected writings, have appeared since his death. He is perhaps the greatest satirist in English literature, and his ruthlessly bleak and misanthropic work stands in stark contrast to the generally milder satire of Dryden, Pope, and Gay. Swift would have been wryly amused that *Gulliver's Travels,* his most famous work, has been bowdlerized as a children's book, with its many sexually suggestive and cynical passages omitted and its elements of fantasy presented merely as an entertaining fable. ✤

Thematic and Structural Analysis

In *Gulliver's Travels* Jonathan Swift overlays satire and parody upon a frame of travel writing as he purports to document Captain Lemuel Gulliver's journeys beyond the known world. A letter from Captain Gulliver to his publisher and cousin, Mr. Sympson, and Sympson's reply preface the text as a narrative device both to reinforce the illusion of reality presented in the accounts and to distance Swift's authorial voice from that of his protagonist. Gulliver claims to publish only at the urging of Sympson and asserts that he no longer has any interest in reforming his countrymen. Yet the narrative itself, in treating scientific, political, and philosophical issues recognizable as contemporary and local, clearly is satire—whose very function is reform.

A map at the beginning of **part one**, "A Voyage to Lilliput," locates the islands of Blefuscu and Lilliput off the coast of Sumatra. The voyage ends in shipwreck, and Gulliver, exhausted after a long swim to shore, falls asleep (**chapter one**). When he awakes he notices first that he has somehow been pinned to the ground. He can move his head no more than two inches left or right, and the sun hurts his eyes. He sees a "human creature" less than six inches high and surmises that as many as forty more are climbing over his body, speaking a language he cannot understand. The Lilliputians shoot him with needlelike arrows as he briefly struggles to free himself. He likens the ferocity of the attack upon him to the effect of "bombs" in European warfare (foreshadowing a different sort of bomb dropped upon him in part four). Gulliver's vision, limited by physical restraints and a blinding sun, introduces the concepts of skewed perspective and intellectual blindness that will become central to the work.

Gulliver convinces the Lilliputians that he is honorable and docile. They feed him enormous quantities of tiny meats and barrels of wine and are so astonished by his tremendous bulk and appetite that they are afraid to cut his bonds, although they are confident that he will not harm them with the hand freed for eating. Sensitive to signs of his digestive processes, the Lilliputians loosen the cords enough for Gulliver to lean upon one side and urinate prodigiously, after which he sleeps for eight hours, the effect of a "sleeping potion in the hogsheads of wine." Such mentions of the most basic bodily functions lend a verisimilitude that will often disgust the reader as it intentionally undermines the intellectual detachment of our stance toward the text—so Swift thus reminds the reader of both the physicality and the arrogance of human nature. Gulliver then details the construction of the machine built to carry him to the capital city, admiring the mathematics of the plans. He is lodged outside the city gates and may walk only to the end of a two-yard chain attached to his leg.

In **chapter two** Gulliver describes the gardenlike countryside, the fields that resemble flower beds, and the trees that at their tallest are just seven feet high. The miniature city looks like a theater backdrop. He perfunctorily records the schedule of his morning bowel movements, completed at the farthest length of his chain and carried off by two servants with wheelbarrows. The emperor and council discuss how they will feed him, and they worry that he will escape his confinement. They consider starving or poisoning him, but the rotting corpse might bring plague. Because Gulliver is merciful to several thugs who attack him, even when given opportunity for revenge, the emperor decides to make the best of it and respond in kind. He orders more comforts for Gulliver and instruction in the Lilliputians' language. But first, Gulliver's pockets are searched and the contents inventoried and described in riddlelike fashion. Observed from the perspective of the Lilliputians, commonplace items are unrecognizable, reminding us that artifacts have meaning only in their proper contexts. But in a private pocket Gulliver has concealed spectacles to correct myopia and a "perspective-glass," or small telescope. His increasing disorientation confirms the novel's constant intimation that the natural eye is unreliable and the scientific eye is inadequate.

In **chapter three** Swift parodies the process of entering into "great employments" at the English court with a description of Lilliputian practices. Candidates for office are trained from youth to dance upon a tightrope, and whoever jumps the highest acquires the desired employment. Furthermore, those already in office must prove their continued worth by occasionally performing as well. In another event, candidates most adept at "leaping and creeping" over or under a stick held parallel to the ground may win blue, red, or green silk threads to wear around their waists.

At last Gulliver gains his freedom. The articles and conditions under which he is released parody formal court language: The emperor is the "delight and terror of the universe," whose garden-patch nation extends to the "extremities of the globe"; the "man-mountain" shall neither come into the city without warning, lie upon crops, nor tread upon "loving subjects." He shall carry court messengers in his pocket as required, destroy the fleet of enemy Blefuscudians preparing to invade Lilliput, assist the royal workmen, and survey the circumference of Lilliput. Ever agreeable and still more curious than uncomfortable, Gulliver submits.

He continues to observe this prosperous and civilized island-nation and to detail his impressions within the conventions of the travel-writing genre, for Gulliver advises the reader that the *Travels* is only part of a greater, and nearly finished, work of scientific and historical rigor. But increasingly *Gulliver's Travels* probes the distinction between perception and reason. The gradual change in Gulliver's character and conception of his own identity as a human will mark his narrative as a novel.

In **chapter four**, lightly veiled comparisons to English politics satirize the gravity with which political factions pursue their agendas. Lilliput is clearly England, and the political parties, the Tramecksan and Slamecksan, representing Tories and Whigs, are distinguishable only by the high or low heels of their shoes. Lilliputian foreign policy parodies contemporary English policy toward France and has its sources in anecdote: As a boy, the emperor's grandfather cut his fingers when breaking open a boiled egg at the large end, so an edict was promptly issued requiring that eggs be broken only at the small end. Rebellions, executions, and exiles ensued, with Big-Endians (or Catholics) fleeing to Blefuscu (France), with which the Little-Endian Lilliput went to war.

In **chapter five**, a well-meaning Gulliver walks across the channel, ties the Blefuscudian warships together, and pulls them into the royal port of Lilliput. But peace is not enough. Gulliver notes the "unmeasurable ambition of princes" and refuses to fulfill the Lilliputian emperor's ambition to vanquish and attach Blefuscu, "compelling that people to break the smaller end of their eggs, by which he would remain sole monarch of the whole world." The emperor of Lilliput never forgives him, despite his honorable service as the negotiator of a peace between the two nations. And Gulliver's dignity is later undercut when he extinguishes a fire in the empress's apartment by three minutes of uninterrupted urination. He is pardoned for violating the law against "making water" within the palace, but the empress is outraged and vows revenge.

Chapter six, in detailing the workings and customs of Lilliputian society, allows Swift to further refine our perspective on size. The Lilliputians see "all objects proper for their view" with "great exactness, but at no great distance." Likewise, Gulliver sees clearly at great distance, but clarity is correspondingly limited when he observes the Lilliputians. Gulliver writes what he observes from a seemingly objective and meticulous viewpoint, which deflects the reader's attention away from the author when he makes obvious comparisons between Lilliputian and English society. The technique serves as Swift's ironic disclaimer—yet to disavow his satire only intensifies its effect.

In **chapter seven** Gulliver describes an intrigue that has been formed against him by several members of the emperor's court for his friendly curiosity about the Blefuscudians, which is regarded as a threat to national security. The conspirators have demanded Gulliver's death, but the emperor is merciful and instead offers the option of blindness. Gulliver sensibly packs his clothes and swims to the royal port of Blefuscu, where he offers his services to the Blefuscudian emperor.

Later, walking along the coast, Gulliver finds a capsized boat fitted to his own proportions. Because he has proven to be more trouble than he is worth, the Blefuscudian emperor grants Gulliver all he needs to make the boat seaworthy and to sustain him, including a small herd of miniature livestock to breed upon his return to England. Gulliver carefully logs the time and circumstances of his departure. Eventually, he is picked up by an English ship, returns home, and regains normal perspective. In England Gulliver exhibits his livestock as curiosities and sells them at great profit before—yielding to his "insatiable desire" to see other countries and having carefully provided for his family—he sails again on a merchant ship.

Part two, "A Voyage to Brobdingnag," takes Gulliver to a peninsular country north of California. Left behind when the ship stops for fresh water, Gulliver finds himself in a position converse to that in Lilliput, for this place is inhabited by giants. A field hand puts Gulliver in his pocket and carries him to his employer, a "substantial farmer," who becomes convinced that Gulliver "must be a rational creature" and so takes him home. The farmer's wife is at first frightened of Gulliver, as if he were "a toad or a spider," but later grows "extremely tender." When she nurses her infant, Gulliver is horrified by the sight of her monstrous, six-foot breast, whose coarse and mottled skin nauseates him but causes him to reflect upon how the fair skin of English women would appear under a magnifying glass, sensing correctly that proportion and perspective determine beauty. He tries to adjust his thinking and makes aesthetic allowances for the sixty-foot farmer, whom he adjudges "very well proportioned." He communicates to the woman that he must attend to certain "necessities of nature" and hides in sorrel leaves to do so. His shame is conspicuous here, where he causes no offense. In Lilliput, where the threat to public health and sensibility was monumental, he was tidy but shameless. His unapologetic physicality in Lilliput was a sign of his innate superiority, and his shame is a sign of his weakness and insignificance in Brobdingnag. Although Gulliver apologizes to his reader for including such details, he declares that they should help a philosopher "to enlarge his thoughts and imagination," by tempering lofty speculations with the truth of one's physical being.

In **chapter two** the farmer's nine-year-old daughter takes motherly charge of the doll-like Gulliver, who names his new keeper Glumdalclitch (Little Nurse). The farmer exhibits him throughout the country, but when Gulliver's good health is exhausted, the farmer sells him to the queen, and Glumdalclitch stays as his keeper (**chapter three**). The king is not at first impressed with this new curiosity, thinking Gulliver may be only a *splacknuck* (a small animal). But when he discerns that Gulliver is a rational being, he calls in three scholars to examine him, and they conclude that Gulliver is not equipped to survive in the world. Because his size is "beyond all degrees of comparison," the scholars decide that he is a *lusus naturae* (freak of nature). Gulliver compares their method of investigation to that of European scientists and philosophers who ignorantly consign to categories what they do not understand.

Through his own distorted perspective, Gulliver describes dinner with the queen and two princesses, where he is appalled and disgusted by the amount of food these giants consume, by the size of their utensils, and by the sight and sound of their eating, forgetting the similar impression he himself had made upon the tiny Lilliputians. Although *Gulliver's Travels* describes the world through various perspectives, Gulliver's failure to compare differences reminds us that one perspective does not necessarily inform another.

Gulliver proudly describes for the prince the society and government of England (**chapter three**). Amused, the prince remarks "how contemptible a thing [is] human grandeur, which could be mimicked by such diminutive insects" as Gulliver. He of course is humiliated, but the Brobdingnagian perspective begins to persuade him that both he and England may indeed appear ridiculous. As he stands upon the queen's hand and both gaze into a mirror, he imagines himself becoming ever smaller. In Brobdingnag he has been put in the care of a little girl, set upon by rats and unpleasant little boys, abused by a dwarf, terrorized by insects and birds, stroked, prodded, and placed upon the dinner table like a potato. Gulliver is thoroughly dehumanized, and English society seems to resemble a traveling show. He does not abandon his investigative purpose, however, and continues his close observations of the country, noting that he later supplied evidence of these adventures to the Royal Society (**chapter four**).

Sustaining a scientific tone, Gulliver, with his visual perspicuity, magnifies human imperfections to loathsome proportions. Nothing can match the image of lice rooting their swinelike snouts into beggars' clothes. But the grandeur of the town's architecture and artifacts restores Gulliver to his traveler's love of observation and detail.

By **chapter five** Glumdalclitch seems to be losing interest in Gulliver's constant companionship, and he himself wishes for some solitude. Although the child always leaves him in a safe place, he lives dangerously. He is carried in the mouth of a dog in the garden, he does battle with a linnet (a type of finch), and a servant nearly drowns him. Among the antic incidents, Gulliver juxtaposes an edited account of sexual dalliance with one of a public execution. The maids of honor strip him naked and use him for sexual purposes "in proportion" to his "littleness." Repelled, he clings to memories of normal perspective and aesthetic ideals of feminine sweetness. After this disturbing episode, Gulliver witnesses and graphically describes the beheading of a murderer. Shortly after, he is suckled and force-fed by a pet monkey. The monkey mimics the human, suggesting to the reader that while to the Brobdingnagians Gulliver is not as human as they, to the monkey he is too human. Gulliver, at least, still seems sure of his own humanity and of the integrity of England, although he remarks upon his isolation among "those who are out of all degree of equality or comparison" with himself, echoing the king's scholars. The chapter concludes with a walk in the country and an unsuccessful leap over cow dung.

In **chapters six and seven**, Gulliver and the king of Brobdingnag compare their nations' governments. Gulliver offers a formal and dignified panegyric on the English parliament, clergy, courts, and military, but the king is scornful. The last century of English history seems to him merely a chaotic and senseless brawl among a "pernicious race of little odious vermin." Gulliver disdains the king's judgment as the "prejudices" and "narrowness of thinking" to be expected from such an isolated nation and unlikely in the "politer countries of Europe."

After a mishap in which, at the shore, Gulliver is snatched by a bird while sleeping in the box where he is kept, he finds himself aboard a ship of the usual scale, and with Englishmen (**chapter eight**). They sail to England, where Gulliver attributes to "the great power of habit and prejudice" the fact that home and family seem to him as if in miniature. All think he has lost his wits.

"A Voyage to Laputa, Balnibarbi, Glubbdubdrib, Luggnagg, and Japan" composes **part three**, which opens with a map showing a crowded and irregular coastline at the edge of the known world. Thrown off his ship by pirates, Gulliver reaches an island where the hot sun upon his face evokes the intense sun of Lilliput in the moments before his normal perspective was displaced (**chapter one**). A "vast opaque body" then eclipses the sun, an "island in the air," named Laputa. Swift juxtaposes language of scientific detachment with descriptions of Gulliver's "natural love of life" and "inward motions of joy" to construct one of the novel's oppositional themes that will be central in this episode. Signalling and shouting, Gulliver is noticed by the Laputans, who lower a chain and pull him up.

Gulliver is briefly an object of wonder to the Laputans, who greet him amiably but soon return to their preoccupation with "cogitation" (**chapter two**). Gulliver describes their peculiar processes of vision and discourse: Their heads seem locked to the right or the left, with one eye turned inward and the other gazing up. Servants called "flappers" accompany them to urge necessary conversation by means of balloonlike bladders filled with pebbles, gently struck upon the mouths and ears. For the intellectual and the physical are at odds in Laputa, whose men are so absorbed in the abstractions of mathematics and music that Gulliver claims he has never seen "a more clumsy, awkward, and unhandy people." A tailor, for example, uses sophisticated measuring techniques to make clothes for Gulliver, but, because of a small but crucial miscalculation, they do not fit. Likewise the Laputan men's fears are a catalog of futile worries about earth's vulnerability to remote cosmic events. The women of Laputa, on the other hand, have an "abundance of vivacity," "contemn their husbands," and contrive at every opportunity to escape to Balnibarbi, the world below—which

Gulliver (and perhaps Swift) attributes to "caprices of womankind."

In **chapters three and four** Gulliver describes in scientific terms the physical properties of Laputa and then of Balnibarbi, to which he travels when he decides that the abstracted Laputans have no interest in him. About Balnibarbi and its capital, Lagado, however, Gulliver says that he never saw "a soil so unhappily cultivated, houses so ill contrived and so ruinous, or a people whose countenances and habit expressed so much misery and want." All of this has come about, he learns, because the nation's inhabitants grew obsessed with the ways of their airy neighbors, the Laputans, and so had erected an academy to put all "arts, sciences, languages, and mechanics on a new foot."

In **chapter five** Gulliver visits Lagado's Grand Academy, a parody of England's Royal Society, whose function is scientific investigation and experimentation. Their work includes a "project for extracting sun-beams out of cucumbers" to be stored for bad weather, an "operation to reduce human excrement to its original food," a treatise upon the "malleability of fire," a method for constructing houses from the roof down, a system by which hogs may plow and fertilize fields simultaneously, a proposal for replacing silkworms with spiders, and a gruesomely fatal experiment upon a dog that employs a bellows to cure colic. An experiment in "speculative learning" posits that "the most ignorant person at a reasonable charge" may write books on "philosophy, poetry, politics, law, mathematics, and theology" "without the least assistance from genius or study." At the academy's school of languages, one scheme proposes to "shorten discourse" by making all words into nouns of one syllable, while another is still more reductive in requiring everyone to carry objects that would signify only themselves in conversation. Another idea is to write academic information upon wafers that students may digest and absorb into their brains. Unfortunately, by the "perverseness of lads," the wafer is often regurgitated before becoming knowledge. Whether this is a satire more of students or of desperate pedagogy, Swift does not reveal.

In **chapter six** Gulliver continues his account of the academy's projects before leaving Lagado for a short voyage to Glubbdubdrib, which is governed by magicians waited upon by spirits of the dead (**chapters seven and eight**). Here Gulliver is permitted to call up spirits he wishes to see, among them Homer, Alexander the Great, and Caesar. But he is disappointed by many of the historical figures he meets, and his cynicism about historians—"prostitute writers"—grows intense. Although Gulliver continues to protest that his account is not a criticism of England, traceable allusions to political intrigue and incompetence prove otherwise. He concludes chapter eight by lamenting the degeneration of the English people, who, compared to the "English yeomen of the old stamp," have been morally corrupted by the seductiveness of power and money and physically rotted by "the pox."

Gulliver then travels to the island kingdom of Luggnagg (**chapter nine**), where "court style" is both ritualistic and perverse. To approach the king, Gulliver must crawl upon his belly and lick the dust off the floor. When he describes the king's method of putting noblemen to death by poisoning the dust, he comments only that he "cannot altogether approve" of the practice. After all, it is considered a "gentle indulgent" death, and the king is kind enough to have the floor thoroughly washed afterward, he explains.

The immortal Struldbruggs are Luggnagg's most remarkable citizens (**chapter ten**). Gulliver eagerly anticipates meeting these "living examples of ancient virtue . . . ready to instruct [him] in the wisdom of all former ages," living versions of the specters of Glubbdubdrib. But eternal life does not include eternal youth, and living forever in old age makes the Struldbruggs covet both "diverting vices" and death. We cannot seem to learn from history, as chapter seven shows us, but neither would outliving it bring wisdom.

After a brief visit to Japan (**chapter eleven**), Gulliver returns to England before setting out on his final adventure, "A Voyage to the Country of the Houyhnhnms" (**part four**). Cast onto an unknown island west of Madagascar, Gulliver hides behind a thicket to observe several hideous and deformed animals with buff-colored and patchily haired bodies, later identified as

Yahoos (**chapter one**). He cannot yet acknowledge their recognizably human attributes, saying that he has never seen "so disagreeable an animal, or one against which [he] naturally conceived so strong an antipathy." In one of the novel's most disturbing episodes, Gulliver is approached by one of the creatures and strikes it, inciting the "brood" to climb into a tree and "discharge their excrements" upon his head: a brilliantly reductive image of European warfare. But suddenly the creatures run away, and Gulliver discovers that the approach of horses has caused their flight. Yet the horses' resistance to his proprietary attentions and their own intense interest in him and his clothing lead Gulliver to conclude that they may be magicians. He asks if one of them might carry him to civilization in exchange for some trinkets. But these are not beasts of burden: They are the Houyhnhnms (pronounced *whin*ums, in imitation of the neighing of horses) and are the dominant species in this realm. Gulliver accordingly walks to their city.

In **chapter two** Gulliver idiotically persists in offering toys to the Houyhnhnms—"two knives, three bracelets of false pearl, a small looking glass and a bead necklace"—taking the horses to be the intelligent servants of human masters. But having been led to a building in which he is shown to a "very comely mare" who appears disgusted by him, he is mortified to find himself then physically compared by the Houyhnhnm to one of the "animals" he had earlier met. To his further horror, Gulliver now observes "in this abominable animal" a perfect human figure. The Yahoos are natural men enslaved by their unmediated passions, from which civilization—any civilization—protects us. In Houyhnhnmland Gulliver must therefore struggle to differentiate himself from these creatures, taking pains to learn the language and to conceal his Yahoo-like body with clothing, and naming the Houyhnhnm his master (**chapter three**).

Having been often asked by his master to tell his story, Gulliver begins, but with the fear that the Houyhnhnm will not believe his account. This trepidation leads to a discussion of the concept of speech—and, on another level, novelistic or fictive speech (**chapter four**). "[T]he use of speech [is] to make us understand one another" through "facts," says the Houyhnhnm. But by saying "the thing which [is] not" (the

Houyhnhnms' only term for falsehood), we may believe "a thing black when it is white, and short when it is long." This both calls into question the narrative as a whole—and, paradoxically, reinforces it. The Houyhnhnms have no conception of fiction or irony, nor even any words for "[p]ower, government, war, law, punishment"—none of which is necessary in their contemplative, rational land.

In **chapters four through seven** Gulliver describes the political, religious, and social complexities of English and European life, wryly remarking that England is "governed by a female man . . . called queen." Gulliver struggles to put into words the nature of his species, but European wars, the actions of monarchs, and the general weaknesses of humans are nearly incomprehensible to a Houyhnhnm. "[W]hen a creature pretending to reason could be capable of such enormities," Gulliver's master says, he dreads "lest the corruption of that faculty might be worse than brutality itself."

In **chapter eight** Gulliver mingles with the dreadful Yahoos, intent on learning more about them. To his mortification, he is molested while bathing by an eleven-year-old female Yahoo and is compelled to accept her attraction to him as proof of their sameness. This episode shockingly contrasts human depravity to the Houyhnhnms' virtue, which Gulliver then eulogizes, likening their philosophy to the "sentiments of Socrates, as Plato delivers them." They live a utopian ideal in which friendship is the true expression of love and marriage is a practical match for producing offspring and lifelong companionship; all children are educated alike in "temperance, industry, exercise, and cleanliness"; all want is peacefully eliminated by action of a representative government. Even in dying, they maintain an ideal absence of fear and passion: Where the Struldbruggs presented an agonizing and inconclusive lesson on death for the Luggnaggians, the Houyhnhnms placidly "retire to the first mother," and the survivors neither regret nor mourn. Gulliver promises to reveal more in another book, soon to be published (**chapter nine**).

After three contented years among the Houyhnhnms—during which Gulliver goes so far in his admiration of his masters that he imitates their gait and speech—he eventually, because his Yahoo-ness is undeniable, is asked to leave. Reluctantly he constructs a canoe (made largely of the skins of Yahoos) and departs (**chapter ten**). Arriving at another island, he is chased back into the sea by unfriendly natives (**chapter eleven**). Although he notices the sail of a ship in the distance, he hides, for the prospect of resuming life among European Yahoos is more distasteful than taking his chances among savages. Eventually he boards a Portuguese ship whose captain, Don Pedro, at last believes Gulliver's strange story and helps reacclimate him to life among humans. But when Gulliver returns to England, where he is warmly received by his family, he is disgusted. When he considers that he has produced offspring by "one of the Yahoo-species," his shame is unbearable, and when the "odious" creature kisses him, he faints. Only by spending four hours each day with two stallions he has purchased does Gulliver endure his return to life among Yahoos.

In the bitter conclusion to *Gulliver's Travels,* the oppositions that construct the novel—its fictive premise yet its satirical purpose, its conflicts posed by perspective and vision—are fully realized. Gulliver declares that his object has been "to inform, and not to amuse" the reader. He claims that the influence of the noble Houyhnhnms has made it impossible for him to lie, so that his work is therefore true, and he, "an author perfectly blameless." He excuses himself to return to his project of looking at his reflection until he may again become accustomed to the sight of the human face. ✤

—*Tenley Williams*
New York University

List of Characters

Lemuel Gulliver is the protagonist and only definable character of the novel. He begins his story as a nimble survivor—curious, resourceful, and ever an Englishman. He behaves responsibly toward his wife and children and is confident that England—which he discusses at every opportunity—is a place of reason and integrity. Gulliver assumes the role of an explorer in the isolated nations he discovers, and he intends to enlighten the inhabitants with knowledge of superior English institutions. Instead, his confidence in the human capacity for reason and in the rectitude of English government is gradually destroyed as he is forced to consider human nature and European society from very different perspectives. He is, at last, unable to resolve or accept the tension between the baseness of human nature and the illusion of civilization. In the course of his four voyages he changes from an optimistic and adventurous young surgeon and travel writer into a dour, antisocial eccentric. ✣

Critical Views

Jonathan Swift on the Purpose of Gulliver's Travels

[Jonathan Swift's most important statement on the purpose behind the writing of *Gulliver's Travels* occurs in a letter to Alexander Pope in late 1725, just as he was finishing the novel. Here, Swift states that his chief aim is to "vex" the human race, which he hates in its totality, although he singles out worthy individuals for his affection.]

I have employd my time (besides ditching) in finishing correcting, amending, and Transcribing my Travells, in four parts Compleat newly Augmented, and intended for the press when the world shall deserve them, or rather when a Printer shall be found brave enough to venture his Eares, I like your Schemes of our meeting after Distresses and dispertions but the chief end I propose to my self in all my labors is <u>to vex the world</u> rather <u>then divert it</u>, and if I could compass that designe without hurting my own person or Fortune I would be the most Indefatigable writer you have ever seen without reading I am exceedingly pleased that you have done with Translations Lord Treasurer Oxford often lamented that a rascaly World should lay you under a Necessity of Misemploying your Genius for so long a time. But since you will now be so much better employd when you think of the World give it one lash the more at my Request. I have ever hated all Nations professions and Communityes and all my love is towards individualls for instance I hate the tribe of Lawyers, but I love Councellor such a one, Judge such a one for so with Physicians (I will not Speak of my own Trade) Soldiers, English, Scotch, French; and the rest but principally I hate and detest that animal called man, although I hartily love John, Peter, Thomas and so forth. this is the system upon which I have governed my self many years (but do not tell) and so I shall go on till I have done with them I have got Materials Towards a Treatis proving the falsity of that Definition *animal rationale* ⟨a rational animal⟩; and to show it should be only *rationis capax* ⟨capable of reason⟩. Upon this great foundation of Misanthropy (though not Timons manner)

25

The whole building of my Travells is erected: And I never will have peace of mind till all honest men are of my Opinion: by Consequence you are to embrace it immediatly and procure that all who deserve my Esteem may do so too. The matter is so clear that it will admit little dispute. nay I will hold a hundred pounds that you and I agree in the Point.
        —Jonathan Swift, Letter to Alexander Pope (29 September 1725), *The Correspondence of Jonathan Swift,* ed. Harold Williams (Oxford: Clarendon Press, 1963), Vol. 3, pp. 102–3

JOHN GAY ON THE CONTEMPORARY REACTIONS TO *GULLIVER'S TRAVELS*

[John Gay (1685–1732), a British poet and dramatist best known for *The Beggar's Opera* (1728), was an associate of Swift's from the time they were members of the Scriblerus Club in 1714. In the following letter to Swift, Gay gives an impression of contemporary readers' reactions to *Gulliver's Travels:* Since it was published anonymously, there was much speculation as to authorship, and many readers criticized its satire on humanity as being too harsh.]

About ten days ago a book was published here of the travels of one Gulliver, which has been the conversation of the whole town ever since: the whole impression sold in a week, and nothing is more diverting than to hear the different opinions people give of it, though all agree in liking it extremely. It is generally said that you are the author; but I am told, the bookseller declares, he knows not from what hand it came. From the highest to the lowest it is universally read, from the cabinet-council to the nursery. The politicians to a man agree, that it is free from particular reflections, but that the satire on general societies of men is too severe. Not but we now and then meet with people of greater perspicuity, who are in search for particular applications in every leaf; and it is highly probable we shall have keys published to give light into Gulliver's design. Lord ⟨Bolingbroke⟩ is the person who least approves it, blaming it as a design of evil consequence to depreciate human nature, at which it cannot be wondered that he takes most offence, being himself the most accomplished of his species, and so losing more than any other of that praise which is due both to the dignity and virtue of a man. Your friend, my Lord Harcourt, commends it very much, though he thinks in some places the matter too far carried. The Duchess Dowager of Marlborough is in raptures at it; she says she can dream of nothing else since she read it; she declares that she has now found out, that her whole life has been lost in caressing the worst part of mankind, and treating the best as her foes; and that if she knew Gulliver, though he had been the worst enemy she ever had, she should give up her present acquaintance for his friendship. You may see by this, that you are not much injured by being supposed the author of this piece. If you are, you have disobliged us, and two or three of your best friends, in not giving us the least hint of it while you were with us; and in particular Dr. Arbuthnot, who says it is ten thousand pities he had not known it, he could have added such abundance of things upon every subject. Among lady critics, some have found out that Mr. Gulliver had a particular malice to maids of honour. Those of them who frequent the Church, say, his design is impious, and that it is an insult on Providence depreciating the works of the Creator. Notwithstanding, I am told the Princess has read it with great pleasure. As to other critics, they think the flying island is the least entertaining; and so great an opinion the town have of the impossibility of Gulliver's writing at all below himself, it is agreed that part was not writ by the same hand, though this has its defenders too. It has passed Lords and Commons, *nemine contradicente* ⟨with no one contradicting⟩; and the whole town, men, women, and children are quite full of it.

    —John Gay, Letter to Jonathan Swift (17 November 1726), *The Correspondence of Alexander Pope,* ed. George Sherburn (Oxford: Clarendon Press, 1956), Vol. 2, pp. 413–14

Sir Walter Scott on the Voyage to the Land of the Houyhnhnms

[Sir Walter Scott (1771–1832), the prolific Scottish author of romantic novels, drama, and verse, was also an important critic and essayist. He frequently contributed to the *Edinburgh Review,* the *Quarterly Review,* and *Encyclopaedia Britannica.* He wrote biographies of John Dryden (1808) and Jonathan Swift (1814) in conjunction with editing their collected works. In this extract from the latter biography, Scott takes offense at Swift's portrayal of human nature in the final section of *Gulliver's Travels.*]

The Voyage to the Land of the Houyhnhnms is a composition an editor of Swift must ever consider with pain. The source of such a diatribe against human nature could only be, that fierce indignation which he has described in his epitaph as so long gnawing his heart. Dwelling in a land where he considered the human race as divided between petty tyrants and oppressed slaves, and being himself a worshipper of that freedom and independence which he beheld daily trampled upon, the unrestrained violence of his feelings drove him to loathe the very species by whom such iniquity was done and suffered. To this must be added, his personal health, broken and worn down by the recurring attacks of a frightful disorder; his social comfort destroyed by the death of one beloved object, and the daily decay and peril of another; his life decayed into autumn, and its remainder, after so many flattering and ambitious prospects, condemned to a country which he disliked, and banished from that in which he had formed his hopes, and left his friendships:—when all these considerations are combined, they form some excuse for that general misanthropy which never prevented a single deed of individual benevolence. Such apologies are personal to the author, but there are also excuses for the work itself. The picture of the Yahoos, utterly odious and hateful as it is, presents to the reader a moral use. It was never designed as a representation of mankind in the state to which religion, and even the lights of nature, encourage men to aspire, but of that to which our species is degraded by the wilful subservience of mental qualities to animal instincts, of man, such as he may be found in the degraded ranks of every society, when brutalized by ignorance and gross vice. In this view, the more coarse and disgusting the picture, the more impressive is the moral to be derived from it, since, in proportion as an individual indulges in sensuality, cruelty, or avarice, he approaches in resemblance to the detested Yahoo.

It cannot, however, be denied, that even a moral purpose will not justify the nakedness with which Swift has sketched this horrible outline of mankind degraded to a bestial state; since a moralist ought to hold, with the Romans, that crimes of atrocity should be exposed when punished, but those of flagitious impurity concealed. In point of probability, too, for there are degrees of probability proper even to the wildest fiction, the fourth part of Gulliver is inferior to the three others. Giants and pigmies the reader can conceive; for, not to mention their being the ordinary machinery of romance, we are accustomed to see, in the inferior orders of creation, a disproportion of size between those of the same generic description, which may parallel (among some reptile tribes at least) even the fiction of Gulliver. But the mind rejects, as utterly impossible, the supposition of a nation of horses placed in houses which they could not build, fed with corn which they could neither sow, reap, nor save, possessing cows which they could not milk, depositing that milk in vessels which they could not make, and, in short, performing a hundred purposes of rational and social life, for which their external structure altogether unfits them.
—Sir Walter Scott, *The Life of Jonathan Swift* (1814), *Miscellaneous Prose Works* (Edinburgh: A. & C. Black, 1851–57), Vol. 2, pp. 297–99

William Hazlitt on Swift's Supposed Misanthropy

[William Hazlitt (1778–1830) was one of the most acute critics and essayists of the early nineteenth century. Among his important works are *Characters of Shakespear's Plays* (1817), *Lectures on the English*

Poets (1818), and a moving account of his love for a coquette, *Liber Amoris* (1823). In this extract, Hazlitt defends Swift from charges of misanthropy by claiming that *Gulliver's Travels* is simply a keen and uncompromising display of the moral failings of humanity.]

Whether the excellence of *Gulliver's Travels* is in the conception or the execution, is of little consequence; the power is somewhere, and it is a power that has moved the world. The power is not that of big words and vaunting common places. Swift left these to those who wanted them; and has done what his acuteness and intensity of mind alone could enable any one to conceive or to perform. His object was to strip empty pride and grandeur of the imposing air which external circumstances throw around them; and for this purpose he has cheated the imagination of the illusions which the prejudices of sense and of the world put upon it, by reducing every thing to the abstract predicament of size. He enlarges or diminishes the scale, as he wishes to shew the insignificance or the grossness of our overweening self-love. That he has done this with mathematical precision, with complete presence of mind and perfect keeping, in a manner that comes equally home to the understanding of the man and of the child, does not take away from the merit of the work or the genius of the author. He has taken a new view of human nature, such as a being of a higher sphere might take of it; he has torn the scales from off his moral vision; he has tried an experiment upon human life, and gifted its pretensions from the alloy of circumstances; he has measured it with a rule, has weighed it in a balance, and found it, for the most part, wanting and worthless—in substance and in shew. Nothing solid, nothing valuable is left in his system but virtue and wisdom. What a libel is this upon mankind! What a convincing proof of misanthropy! What presumption and what *malice prepense,* to shew men what they are, and to teach them what they ought to be! What a mortifying stroke aimed at national glory, is that unlucky incident of Gulliver's wading across the channel and carrying off the whole fleet of Blefuscu! After that, we have only to consider which of the contending parties was in the right. What a shock to personal vanity is given in the account of Gulliver's nurse Glumdalclitch! Still, notwithstanding the disparagement to her personal charms, her good-nature remains the same amiable quality as before. I cannot see the harm, the misanthropy, the immoral and degrading tendency of this. The moral lesson is as fine as the intellectual exhibition is amusing. It is an attempt to tear off the mask of imposture from the world; and nothing but imposture has a right to complain of it. It is, indeed, the way with our quacks in morality to preach up the dignity of human nature, to pamper pride and hypocrisy with the idle mockeries of the virtues they pretend to, and which they have not: but it was not Swift's way to cant morality, or any thing else; nor did his genius prompt him to write unmeaning panegyrics on mankind!

I do not, therefore, agree with the estimate of Swift's moral or intellectual character, given by an eminent critic, who does not seem to have forgotten the party politics of Swift. I do not carry my political resentments so far back: I can at this time of day forgive Swift for having been a Tory. I feel little disturbance (whatever I might think of them) at his political sentiments, which died with him, considering how much else he has left behind him of a more solid and imperishable nature! If he had, indeed, (like some others) merely left behind him the lasting infamy of a destroyer of his country, or the shining example of an apostate from liberty, I might have thought the case altered.
—William Hazlitt, *Lectures on the English Poets* (1818), *The Complete Works of William Hazlitt,* ed. P. P. Howe (London: J. M. Dent & Sons, 1930), Vol. 5, pp. 110–11

JAMES RUSSELL LOWELL ON SWIFT'S SELF-HATRED

[James Russell Lowell (1819–1891), an important American poet, was also a noted critic and reviewer, having written such volumes of critical essays as *Among My Books* (1870) and *My Study Windows* (1871). In the following extract, taken from a review of John Forster's biography of Swift, Lowell believes that

Swift's misanthropy is a product of Swift's hatred of himself.]

He despised mankind because he found something despicable in Jonathan Swift, as he makes Gulliver hate the Yahoos in proportion to their likeness with himself. He had more or less consciously sacrificed self-respect for that false consideration which is paid to a man's accidents; he had preferred the vain pomp of being served on plate, as no other "man of his level" in Ireland was, to being happy with the woman who had sacrificed herself to his selfishness, and the independence he had won turned out to be only a morose solitude after all. "Money," he was fond of saying, "is freedom," but he never learned that self-denial is freedom with the addition of self-respect. With a hearty contempt for the ordinary objects of human ambition, he could yet bring himself for the sake of them to be the obsequious courtier of three royal strumpets. How should he be happy who had defined happiness to be "the perpetual possession of being well deceived," and who could never be deceived himself? It may well be doubted whether what he himself calls "that pretended philosophy which enters into the depth of things and then comes gravely back with informations and discoveries that in the inside they are good for nothing," be of so penetrative an insight as it is apt to suppose, and whether the truth be not rather that to the empty all things are empty. Swift's diseased eye had the miscroscopic quality of Gulliver's in Brobdignag, and it was the loathsome obscenity which this revealed in the skin of things that tainted his imagination when it ventured on what was beneath. But with all Swift's scornful humor, he never made the pitiful mistake of his shallow friend Gay that life was a jest. To his nobler temper it was always profoundly tragic, and the salt of his sarcasm was more often, we suspect, than with most humorists distilled out of tears. The lesson is worth remembering that *his* apples of Sodom, like those of lesser men, were plucked from boughs of his own grafting.
 —James Russell Lowell, "Forster's Life of Swift," *Nation,* 20 April 1876, p. 265

LESLIE STEPHEN ON THE YAHOOS AND THE HOUYHNHNMS

[Leslie Stephen (1832–1904), a leading British critic and the father of Virginia Woolf, wrote such works as *Hours in a Library* (1874–79) and *History of English Thought in the Eighteenth Century* (1876). In this extract from his study of Swift, Stephen focuses on the Yahoos and the Houyhnhnms, whom he believes to be representations of the worst and the best traits of humanity.]

The Yahoo is the embodiment of the bestial element in man; and Swift in his wrath takes the bestial for the predominating element. The hideous, filthy, lustful monster yet asserts its relationship to him in the most humiliating fashion; and he traces in its conduct the resemblance to all the main activities of the human being. Like the human being, it fights and squabbles for the satisfaction of its lust, or to gain certain shiny yellow stones; it befouls the weak and fawns upon the strong with loathsome compliance; shows a strange love of dirt, and incurs diseases by laziness and gluttony. Gulliver gives an account of his own breed of Yahoos, from which it seems that they differ from the subjects of the Houyhnhnms only by showing the same propensities on a larger scale; and justifies his master's remark, that all their institutions are owing to "gross defects in reason, and by consequence in virtue." The Houyhnhnms, meanwhile, represent Swift's Utopia: they prosper and are happy, truthful, and virtuous, and therefore able to dispense with lawyers, physicians, ministers and all the other apparatus of an effete civilization. It is in this doctrine, as I may observe in passing, that Swift falls in with Godwin and the revolutionists, though they believed in human perfectibility, while they traced every existing evil to the impostures and corruptions essential to all systems of government. Swift's view of human nature is too black to admit of any hopes of their millennium.

The full wrath of Swift against his species shows itself in this ghastly caricature. It is lamentable and painful, though even here we recognize the morbid perversion of a noble wrath against oppression. One other portrait in Swift's gallery demands a moment's notice. No poetic picture in Dante or

Milton can exceed the strange power of his prose description of the Struldbrugs—those hideous immortals who are damned to an everlasting life of drivelling incompetence. It is a translation of the affecting myth of Tithonus into the repulsive details of downright prose. It is idle to seek for any particular moral from these hideous phantoms of Swift's dismal *Inferno.* They embody the terror which was haunting his imagination as old age was drawing upon him. The sight, he says himself, should reconcile a man to death. The mode of reconciliation is terribly characteristic. Life is but a weary business at best; but, at least, we cannot wish to drain so repulsive a cup to the dregs, when even the illusions which cheered us at moments have been ruthlessly destroyed. Swift was but too clearly prophesying the melancholy decay into which he was himself to sink.
—Leslie Stephen, *Swift* (New York: Harper & Brothers, 1882), pp. 179–81

Sir Walter Raleigh on the Strengths of Swift's Satire

[Sir Walter Raleigh (1861–1922), a significant British lecturer and critic, taught at Liverpool University and Glasgow University before becoming the first holder of the chair of English literature at Oxford University. His publications include *Style* (1897), *Milton* (1900), and *Shakespeare* (1907). In this extract, Raleigh maintains that the greatness of *Gulliver's Travels* lies in its realism and in the naive honesty with which Gulliver renders his verdicts on humanity.]

Swift's great work, after storming the outposts of human policy and human learning, breaks at last in a torrent of contempt and hatred on the last stronghold of humanity itself. The strength of Swift's work as a contribution to the art of fiction lies in the portentous gravity and absolute mathematical consistency wherewith he develops the consequences of his modest assumptions. In the quality of their realism the voyages to Lilliput and Brobdingnag are much superior to the two later

and more violent satires: he was better fitted to ridicule the politics of his time than to attack the "men of Gresham," of whose true aims and methods he knew little or nothing; and the imagination stumbles at many of the details of the last book. But the wealth of illustration whereby he maintains the interest of his original conception of pigmies and giants is eternally surprising and delightful. Defoe could have made of Captain Lemuel Gulliver a living man; he, too, could have recorded with the minutest circumstance of date and place the misadventures and actions of his hero: it may well be doubted whether he could have carried into an unreal world that literalism, accuracy of proportion, and imaginative vividness of detail wherewith Swift endows it. The cat in Brobdingnag makes a noise in purring like "a dozen Stocking-weavers at work;" Gulliver is clad in clothes of the thinnest silk, "not much thicker than an English blanket, very cumbersome, till I was accustomed to them;" the sailing-boat wherein he shows his skill in navigation is taken, when he has done, and hung upon a nail to dry. These are the sources of the pleasure that children take in the book; the astonishing strokes of savage satire that are its chief attraction for their elders derive most of their force from the imperturbable innocence and quietude of manner that disarms suspicion. Like Iago, Gulliver is a fellow "of exceeding honesty," and he goes about his deadly work the better for his bluntness and scrupulous pretence of veracity. But the design of the book forbids its classification among works of pure fiction; it is enough to remark that in *Gulliver* realism achieved one of the greatest of its triumphs before its ultimate conquest of the novel.
—Sir Walter Raleigh, *The English Novel* (New York: Scribners, 1899), pp. 137–38

F. R. Leavis on *Gulliver's Travels* as a Travel Book

[F. R. Leavis (1895–1978) was a professor of English at Cambridge University and a pioneering critic of the first half of the twentieth century. He wrote *Revaluation* (1936), *The Great Tradition* (1948), and many other books and was the founder of the critical journal *Scrutiny.* In this extract, Leavis believes that the chief virtue of *Gulliver's Travels* for adults is exactly what appeals to children—its vivid descriptions of imaginary lands.]

To direct the attention upon Swift's irony gives, I think, the best chance of dealing adequately, without deviation or confusion, with what is essential in his work. But it involves also (to anticipate an objection) a slight to the classical status of *Gulliver's Travels,* a book which, though it may represent Swift's most impressive achievement in the way of complete creation—the thing achieved and detached—does not give the best opportunities for examining his irony. And *Gulliver's Travels,* one readily agrees, hasn't its classical status for nothing. But neither is it for nothing that, suitably abbreviated, it has become a classic for children. What for the adult reader constitutes its peculiar force—what puts it in so different a class from *Robinson Crusoe*—resides for the most part in the fourth book (to a less extent in the third). The adult may re-read the first two parts, as he may *Robinson Crusoe,* with great interest, but his interest, apart from being more critically conscious, will not be of a different order from the child's. He will, of course, be aware of an ingenuity of political satire in *Lilliput,* but the political satire is, unless for historians, not very much alive to-day. And even the more general satire characteristic of the second book will not strike him as very subtle. His main satisfaction, a great deal enhanced, no doubt, by the ironic seasoning, will be that which Swift, the student of the *Mariner's Magazine* and of travellers' relations, aimed to supply in the bare precision and the matter-of-fact realness of his narrative.

But what in Swift is most important, the disturbing characteristic of his genius, is a peculiar emotional intensity; that which, in *Gulliver,* confronts us in the Struldbrugs and the Yahoos. It is what we find ourselves contemplating when elsewhere we examine his irony. To lay the stress upon an emotional intensity should be matter of commonplace: actually, in routine usage, the accepted word for Swift is 'intellectual.' We are told, for

instance, that his is pre-eminently 'intellectual satire' (though we are not told what satire is). For this formula the best reason some commentators can allege is the elaboration of analogies—their 'exact and elaborate propriety'—in *Gulliver*. But a muddled perception can hardly be expected to give a clear account of itself; the stress on Swift's 'intellect' (Mr. Herbert Read alludes to his 'mighty intelligence') registers, it would appear, a confused sense, not only of the mental exercise involved in his irony, but of the habitually critical attitude he maintains towards the world, and of the negative emotions he specializes in.
    —F. R. Leavis, "The Irony of Swift," *Scrutiny* 2, No. 4 (March 1934): 364–65

Ricardo Quintana on Lilliput as a Utopia

[Ricardo Quintana was a professor of English at the University of Wisconsin and a leading scholar on Swift. He wrote *Two Augustans: John Locke and Jonathan Swift* (1978), *Swift: An Introduction* (1979), and *The Mind and Art of Jonathan Swift* (1936), from which the following extract is taken. Here, Quintana discusses the land of Lilliput as Swift's conception of a utopia or ideal realm.]

In addition to the charmingly fantastic quality of this Voyage, its element of political satire, and its reduction of human motives to the mean and contemptible passions displayed by diminutive beings, there is the Utopian theme developed in chapter vi, where the learning, laws, customs, and educational methods of the Lilliputians are set forth in ideal terms. Coming after Gulliver's realistic observations and none too happy experiences, this description is so incongruous as to call for explanation, and we are in fact told that only the original institutions of Lilliput are to be understood and 'not the most scandalous Corruptions into which these People are fallen by the degenerate Nature of Man.' Are we to read these words—and perhaps the entire Utopian sketch—as a sly dig at those writers given to creating impossibly ideal societies? Probably not. Swift had merely manœuvred himself into an awkward position by embodying early material now standing in contradiction to his later representation of the Lilliputians, and was covering up faulty workmanship.

Lilliput's criminal code is a model of simplicity: if an accused man is acquitted, his informer is severely punished; 'They look upon Fraud as a greater Crime than Theft, and therefore seldom fail to punish it with Death'; ingratitude is also a capital crime; and rewards are provided for those who have conspicuously obeyed the laws. Their principles of government are too good to be true—that is, they are precisely those which the English have never had the sense to act upon.

> In chusing Persons for all Employments, they have more Regard to good Morals than to great Abilities: For, since Government is necessary to Mankind, they believe that the common Size of human Understandings, is fitted to some Station or other; and that Providence never intended to make the Management of publick Affairs a Mystery, to be comprehended only by a few Persons of sublime Genius, of which there seldom are three born in an Age: But, they suppose Truth, Justice, Temperance, and the like, to be in every Man's Power; the Practice of which Virtues, assisted by Experience and a good Intention, would qualify any Man for the Service of his Country, except where a Course of Study is required.

Swift opens his discussion of the Lilliputian educational system by observing that 'their Notions relating to the Duties of Parents and Children differ extremely from ours,' and the sub-acid flavour of this remark seasons what follows. Since men and women are joined together like other animals by motives of concupiscence and since their affection for their offspring proceeds from the same natural principle, the Lilliputians reason that a child is under no obligation to its parents for bringing it into the world and that, furthermore, 'Parents are the last of all others to be trusted with the Education of their own Children.' (If there is an unpleasant undertone here,—evidence not of an aversion to children so much as an unhealthy refusal to accept the physical terms of life,—we ought not to miss the ironic accent, not uncommon in the reproaches levelled by perfectly humane bachelors at troublesome brats and over-fond parents.) Public nurseries are maintained in every town and to these all children except those of cottagers and labourers must be sent and at a very early age. Their parents may visit them but twice a year and then for not more than an hour, and although they may kiss their children at meeting and parting, a professor stands by to see that they do not whisper to them 'or use any fondling Expressions, or bring any Presents of Toys, Sweet-meats, and the like.' There are different nurseries for the various social classes, and boys and girls are always sent to separate schools. However, the education given to girls is in almost all respects the same as that for boys, and thus 'the young Ladies there are as much ashamed of being Cowards and Fools, as the Men; and despise all personal Ornaments beyond Decency and Cleanliness.' In these matters they are guided by the maxim 'that among People of Quality, a Wife should be always a reasonable and agreeable Companion, because she cannot always be young.' The meaner families, besides being assessed the usual fee for the education of their children, are obliged to contribute a share of each month's income towards a portion for the child, 'For the *Lilliputians* think nothing can be more unjust, than that People, in Subservience to their own Appetites, should bring Children into the World, and leave the Burthen of supporting them on the Publick.' The children of cottagers and labourers, whose business is only to till and cultivate the soil, are not educated in the public nurseries, though the old and diseased among them are cared for in hospitals with the result that begging is unknown in Lilliput.

In the final pages of the narrative Gulliver returns to civilization and we experience with him the strange sensation of readjusting our sense of proportion to the normal world. But it should be noted that the contrast which is felt is purely and simply a physical one and altogether amusing.

—Ricardo Quintana, *The Mind and Art of Jonathan Swift* (New York: Oxford University Press, 1936), pp. 309–11

DAVID WORCESTER ON THE CHARACTER OF GULLIVER

[David Worcester is the author of *The Art of Satire* (1940), from which the following extract is taken. Here, Worcester studies the character of Gulliver, which he believes to be a constantly shifting perspective that makes it difficult for the reader to follow the direction of the satire.]

Gulliver's Travels is tragic and comic at the same time, as ironical works are apt to be. Gulliver sees and hears things so devastating to the self-respect of man as a rational or a political animal that he must cry, "Lend me a halter or a knife," had he the least spark of philosophy in him. But his naïveté protects him, and the moral cataclysm overwhelms him only after his sojourn among the Houyhnhnms. The reader has a prodigious task to perform if he would follow all the cross-shafts of irony; indeed, it is too great a task for most minds, as the history of Swiftian criticism shows. Not only is it puzzling to follow Gulliver's manner as it changes from ingenuousness to dawning cynicism and at last to disillusioned alienation from all human affairs, but it is often difficult to follow the direction of the satire. To be more specific, Gulliver sometimes laughs at absurdities in Lilliput—genuine absurdities and truly ludicrous, inserted by Swift to support his central fiction. At other times, Gulliver despises foreign absurdities that prove on examination to be slightly distorted versions of absurdities actually to be found in European life. More frequently the imperfections of Gulliver's civilization are ironically assumed to be superior to the manifest excellencies of the civilizations visited. Accordingly, Gulliver is now in the position of a native being examined by foreigners, and now in the position of a traveler observing an exotic culture. It falls to the reader to work out an endless series of implied contrasts and comparisons. He must examine each pair of parallel lines to determine whether they are moving in the same direction or in opposite directions.
—David Worcester, *The Art of Satire* (Cambridge, MA: Harvard University Press, 1940), pp. 104–5

GEORGE ORWELL ON BROBDINGNAG

[George Orwell was the pseudonym of Eric Blair (1903–1950), the author of *Animal Farm* (1945) and *Nineteen Eighty-Four* (1949), two of the most brilliant satires of modern times. Orwell was also a prolific critic, essayist, and reviewer. In the following extract, Orwell, in an imaginary interview with Swift, focuses on the pungent misanthropy of a particular passage in the voyage to Brobdingnag.]

ORWELL: I believe *Gulliver's Travels* has meant more to me than any other book ever written. I can't remember when I first read it, I must have been eight years old at the most, and it's lived with me ever since so that I suppose a year has never passed without my re-reading at least part of it. And yet I can't help feeling that you laid it on a bit too thick. You were too hard on humanity, and on your own country. You even preferred Louis XV's France, which is almost like preferring Hitler's Germany today.

SWIFT: H'm!

ORWELL: For instance, here's a passage that has always stuck in my memory—also stuck in my gizzard, a little. It's at the end of Chapter VI in the Second Book of *Gulliver's Travels*. Gulliver has just given the King of Brobdingnag a long description of life in England. The King listens to him and then picks him up in his hand, strokes him gently and says—wait a moment, I've got the book here. But perhaps you remember the passage yourself.

SWIFT: Oh, ay. 'It does not appear, from all you have said, how any one virtue is required toward the procurement of any one station among you; much less that men were ennobled on account of their virtue; that priests were advanced for their piety or learning, soldiers, for their conduct or valour; judges, for their integrity; senators, for the love of their country; or counsellors for their wisdom. As for yourself (continued the king) who have spent the greatest part of your life in travelling I am well disposed to hope you may hitherto have escaped many vices of your country. But by what I have gathered from your own relation, and the answers I have with much pains wringed and extorted from you, I cannot but conclude the bulk of your natives to be the most pernicious race of little odious vermin that nature ever suffered to crawl upon the surface of the earth.'

ORWELL: I'd allow you 'pernicious' and 'odious' and 'vermin', Dr Swift, but I'm inclined to cavil at 'most'. 'The most pernicious.' Are we in this island really worse than the *rest* of the world?

SWIFT: Not at all. But I know you, better than I know the rest of the world. When I wrote, I went upon the principle that if a lower kind of animal than an Englishman existed, I could not imagine it.

ORWELL: That was two hundred years ago. Surely you must admit that we have made a certain amount of progress since then?

SWIFT: Progress in quantity, yes. The buildings are taller and the vehicles move faster. Human beings are more numerous and commit greater follies. A battle kills a million where it used to kill a thousand. And in the matter of great men, as you still call them, I must admit that your age outdoes mine. Whereas previously some petty tyrant was considered to have reached the highest point of human fame if he laid waste a single province and pillaged half a dozen towns, your great men nowadays can devastate whole continents and reduce entire races of men to the status of slaves.
—George Orwell, "Jonathan Swift: An Imaginary Interview" (1942), *Orwell: The War Broadcasts,* ed. W. J. West (London: Duckworth, 1985), pp. 112–13

SAMUEL H. MONK ON *GULLIVER'S TRAVELS* AS A COMIC MASTERPIECE

[Samuel H. Monk was a critic and scholar who wrote *The Sublime: A Study of Critical Theories in XVIII-*

Century England (1935) and edited Sir William Temple's *Five Miscellaneous Essays* (1963). In the following extract, Monk believes that the comic qualities of *Gulliver's Travels* have been underestimated by critics who have stressed the dark misanthropy of the work.]

A friend once wrote me of having shocked an associate by remarking that he had laughed often on rereading *Gulliver's Travels.* "What should I have done?" he asked me. "Blown out my brains?" I am sure that Swift would have approved my friend's laughter. To conclude that *Gulliver's Travels* expresses despair or that its import is nihilistic is radically to misread the book. All of Swift's satire was written in anger, contempt, or disgust, but it was written to promote self-knowledge in the faith that self-knowledge will lead to right action. Nothing would have bewildered him more than to learn that he had led a reader to the desperate remedy of blowing out his brains. But the book is so often called morbid, so frequently have readers concluded that it is the work of an incipient madman, that I think it worth while to emphasize the gayety and comedy of the voyages as an indication of their author's essential intellectual and spiritual health. True, seventeen years after finishing *Gulliver's Travels,* Swift was officially declared *non compos mentis.* But his masterpiece was written at the height of his powers, and the comic animation of the book as a whole rules out the suspicion of morbidity and mental illness.

We laugh and were meant to laugh at the toy kingdom of the Lilliputians; at the acrobatic skill of the politicians and courtiers; at the absurd jealousy of the diminutive minister who suspects an adulterous relationship between his wife and the giant Gulliver. We laugh at the plight of Gulliver in Brobdingnag: one of the lords of creation, frightened by a puppy, rendered ludicrous by the tricks of a mischievous monkey, in awe of a dwarf; embarrassed by the lascivious antics of the maids of honor; and at last content to be tended like a baby by his girl-nurse. We laugh at the abstractness of the philosophers of Laputa, at the mad experimenters of Balnibarbi. And I am sure that we are right in at least smiling at the preposterous horses, the Houyhnhnms, so limited and so positive in their knowledge and opinions, so skilled in such improbable tasks as threading needles or carrying trays, so complacent in their assurance that they are "the Perfection of Nature." Much of the delight that we take in *Gulliver's Travels* is due to this gay, comic, fanciful inventivness. Swift might well say in the words of Hamlet: "Lay not that flattering unction to your soul/That not your trespass but my madness speaks." Swift did not wish us to blow out our brains; he did wish us to laugh. But beyond the mirth and liveliness are gravity, anger, anxiety, frustration—and he meant us to experience them fully.

For there is an abyss below this fantastic world—the dizzying abyss of corrupt human nature. Swift is the great master of shock. With perfect control of tone and pace, with perfect timing, he startles us into an awareness of this abyss and its implications. We are forced to gaze into the stupid, evil, brutal heart of humanity, and when we do, the laughter that Swift has evoked is abruptly silenced. The surface of the book is comic, but at its center is tragedy, transformed through style and tone into icy irony. Soft minds have found Swift's irony unnerving and depressing and, in self-protection, have dismissed him as a repellent misanthrope. Stronger minds that prefer unpalatable truths to euphoric illusions have found this irony bracing and healthful.
—Samuel H. Monk, "The Pride of Lemuel Gulliver" (1952), *Sewanee Review* 63, No. 1 (Spring 1955): 48–50

Kathleen Williams on the Structure of *Gulliver's Travels*

[Kathleen Williams is a British critic and author of *Spenser's World of Glass: A Reading of* The Faerie Queene (1966) and *Jonathan Swift and the Age of Compromise* (1958), from which the following extract is taken. Here, Williams asserts that *Gulliver's Travels* is not a random collection of fantastic voyages but is structurally unified by the flow of its satire and irony.]

Gulliver's Travels is Swift's most complete and most masterly summing-up of the nature of man and of his proper behavior in a difficult world. As in so much of his writing, he works partly through parody, parody of travel literature and its authors, parody of the conclusions of the philosophic voyagers; but here as in *A Tale of a Tub,* the anti-romantic poems, or the *Modest Proposal,* parody is only a means to a moral end, serving, especially in the fourth voyage, to make Swift's point in the most economical way by a sharp reversal of the findings common in travels to Utopia. The "Voyage to the Houyhnhnms" is so much the most striking and effective that it has often been considered in isolation, but in fact it is the climax towards which the whole work moves. Swift claimed, in his humorous but wholly serious letter to Pope, that the *Travels* in its entirety was built upon the same "great foundation of misanthropy, though not in Timon's manner," and it is true that a consistent purpose is visible throughout. Even the "Voyage to Laputa," once scorned as untidy, superficial, boring, a book of left-overs, can now be seen in its proper eighteenth century context as highly relevant to Swift's general purpose. The whole of *Gulliver's Travels,* though it is timeless in its vision of the unchanging condition of man, is at the same time contemporary, presenting humanity in the particular situation of Swift's scientific, system-making, Deistic, and rationalistic age. Compared with *A Tale of a Tub,* the *Travels* is a model of clarity and order, but it is more inclusive than the earlier work, for Swift's perfect choice of vehicle enables him to deal without confusion, often in the same incident or character, with science, philosophy, politics, morals. The third voyage is conceived in terms of contemporary science, but it has also political connotations and relevance to Swift's primary theme of the proper activity of man; the voyages to Lilliput and Brobdingnag are moral and political, but Swift's chosen allegory of the giants and pygmies, the enormous and the microscopic, has great significance for the new scientific age. Book IV is less concerned with science or with politics, for here we have reached the primary theme itself, and Swift treats openly of the different attitudes to man which underlie differences on the political or scientific level; but the moral lesson, with its basis in Christian tradition, is related to the ideas of Hobbes and Locke,

Shaftesbury and Bolingbroke and Descartes, and the progressive and Deistic perfectionism of the philosophic voyagers. Satiric method can never, in Swift, be considered apart from his theme, but here form and content are even more beautifully integrated than in his other work. The "Voyage to Laputa," it is true, is a partial exception, but even here commentators have in the past exaggerated its untidiness and its episodic quality. Miss Nicolson and Miss Mohler have demonstrated the unity of theme which had been lost to the readers of the nineteenth and twentieth centuries, and it is not, I think, special pleading to suggest that here as in *A Tale of a Tub* an air of confusion and wrongheadedness is part of the theme, for the Laputans have plunged into unreality as delightedly as the author of the *Tale*. Structurally it is perhaps a fault to revert to another and earlier method in the midst of an ostensibly factual and sober work, but the psychological effect of this book, placed as it is before the "Voyage to the Houyhnhnms," is well calculated.
—Kathleen Williams, *Jonathan Swift and the Age of Compromise* (Lawrence: University of Kansas Press, 1958), pp. 154–55

ROBERT C. ELLIOTT ON GULLIVER AS A SATIRIST

[Robert C. Elliott (1914–1981) was a professor of English at Ohio State University and the University of California. He is the author of *The Literary Persona* (1982) and *The Power of Satire* (1960), from which the following extract is taken. Here, Elliott considers Gulliver himself as a satirist distinct from Swift, one who progresses from naive innocence to cynical misanthropy in the course of the novel.]

We must look at some of the formal relations governing the work. Swift gives us little "outside" information about how or when Gulliver wrote the account of his travels. Richard Sympson, the fictive publisher, said to be a relative of Gulliver on his mother's side, writes that he corrected the Captain's papers; and Gulliver himself complains that his manuscript has been tampered with. That is all we know. Within the work itself, however, is evidence that Gulliver composed his memoirs as an elderly man, after he had retired from his unfortunate life on the sea. Several times in the narrative Gulliver looks back in chronological time to previous voyages, bringing his experience from them to bear on a "present" predicament; but he never looks forward specifically to "future" adventures as commentary on what is happening at the moment. Still, it is apparent from casual comments in the early voyages that a whole realm of "future" experience is available to the writer. For example, at the end of Part I Gulliver describes his preparations for shipping out again: "My Daughter *Betty* (who is now well married, and has Children) was then at her Needle-Work." Between "now"—at the time of writing—and "then" lie the years of Gulliver's three subsequent voyages, plus five years which elapse between his final return to England and the composition of the work.

The Gulliver who writes, then, is Gulliver the misanthrope who stuffs his nose with tobacco leaves and keeps a long table between himself and his wife. It is he who "creates" the ship's surgeon—a man capable of longing for the tongue of Demosthenes so that he may celebrate his country in a style equal to its unparalleled merits. Given the emotional and intellectual imbalance of the old seaman, he is remarkably successful in producing an objective portrait of himself as he was in time long past.

The actual, as opposed to the fictive, situation, of course, is that Swift has created two dominant points of view to control the materials of the *Travels:* that of his favorite *ingénu* (the younger Gulliver) and that of the misanthrope. The technique has obvious advantages. An *ingénu* is a superb agent of indirect satire as he roams the world uncritically recording or even embracing the folly which it is the satirist's business to undermine: "*Flimnap,* the Treasurer, is allowed to cut a Caper on the strait Rope, at least an Inch higher than any other Lord in the whole Empire." On the other hand, a misanthrope can develop all the great power of direct, hyperbolic criticism. By allowing Gulliver, an uncritical lover of man, to become an uncritical hater of man, Swift has it both ways.

The technique is not that of the novelist, however. Swift pays little regard to psychological consistency; Gulliver's character can hardly be said to develop; it simply changes. If one takes seriously the premise that Gulliver writes his memoirs after his rebirth, then many passages in the early voyages turn out to be inconsistent and out of character. "There are," says Gulliver of Lilliput, "some Laws and Customs in this Empire very peculiar; and if they were not so directly contrary to those of my own dear Country, I should be tempted to say a little in their Justification." (The laws from Swift's point of view, from the point of view of reason, are excellent.) Here Gulliver is trapped in a conflict between his patriotism and his reason; as he is an *ingénu* his patriotism wins. But note the tense: "I should be tempted"; that is, now—at the time of writing. Given this tense, and given the logic of the controlling situation, it must follow that this is the utterance of Gulliver as he composes the work. At the time he writes, however, Gulliver is committed so irrevocably to the claims of reason that the appeal of patriotism could not possibly have meaning for him—could not, that is, if we assume general consistency in Gulliver's character.
—Robert C. Elliott, *The Power of Satire: Magic, Ritual, Art* (Princeton: Princeton University Press, 1960), pp. 189–91

Claude Rawson on *Gulliver's Travels* as a Parody of a Travel Book

[Claude Rawson is a professor of English at Yale University and the author of many books, including *The Character of Swift's Satire* (1983), *English Satire and the Satiric Tradition* (1984), and *Satire and Sentiment 1660–1830* (1994). In this extract, taken from *Gulliver and the Gentle Reader* (1973), Rawson shows how Swift's parody of a travel book causes the reader of *Gulliver's Travels* to be continually uncertain about the nature of the work.]

We are hardly expected to take *Gulliver's Travels* as a straight (even if possibly mendacious) travel story. But the sea captain who claimed to be 'very well acquainted with Gulliver, but that the printer had Mistaken, that he livd in Wapping, & not in Rotherhith', the old gentleman who searched for Lilliput on the map, the Irish Bishop who said the 'Book was full of improbable lies, and for his part, he hardly believed a word of it' (though some of these readers may have been more *ben trovati* than real) do tell a kind of truth about the work. Swift's whole ironic programme depends on our not being taken in by the travel-book element, but it does require us to be infected with a residual uncertainty about it; and these instances of an over-successful hoax fulfil, extremely, a potential in the work to which all readers must uneasily respond. This is not to accept the simpler accounts of Swiftian betrayal, which suggest that the plain traveller's, or modest proposer's, factuality lulls the reader into a false credulity, and then springs a trap. With Swift, we are always on our guard from the beginning (I believe this is true of sensitive *first* readings as well as later ones), and what surprises us is not the fact of betrayal but its particular form in each case. But if we are on our guard, we do not know what we are guarding against. The travel-book factuality, to which we return at least at the beginning and end of each book (even the end of book IV, in its strange way, sustains and elaborates the pretence), is so insistent, and at its purest so lacking in obvious pointers to a parodic intention, that we really do not know *exactly* how to take it. What saves the ordinary reader from being totally taken in is, obviously, the surrounding context. (The very opening of the narrative, from the 1735 edition onwards, is coloured by the letter to Sympson: but even before 1735 one would have needed to be exceptionally obtuse to think, by the end of the first chapter, that one was still reading a travel-book.) But not being taken in, and knowing the plain style to be parodic, do not save us from being unsure of what is being mocked: travel-books, fictions posing as travel-books, philosophic tales (like *Gulliver* itself) posing as fictions posing as travel-books. Bewilderment is increased by the uncertainty of how much weight to give, moment by moment, to the fact of parody as such and to whatever the style may be mocking, since the parody as we have seen is continuously impregnated with satiric purposes which transcend or exist outside it, but which may still feed on it in subtle ways. And we cannot be sure that some of the plainness is not

meant to be taken straight, not certainly as factual truth, but (in spite of everything) momentarily as realistic fictional trimmings: at least, the style helps to establish the 'character' of the narrator, though this 'character' in turn has more life as the basis of various ironies than as a vivid fictional personality. No accurate account can exhaust the matter, or escape an element of giddy circularity. The proper focus for Swift's precise sober narrative links is paradoxically a blurred focus, because we do not know what to make of all the precision. The accumulation of unresolved doubt that we carry into our reading of more central parts of *Gulliver's Travels* creates, then, not a credulity ripe for betrayal, but a more continuous defensive uneasiness. This undermining of our nervous poise makes us peculiarly vulnerable, in more than the obvious sense, to the more central satiric onslaughts.
—Claude Rawson, *Gulliver and the Gentle Reader: Studies in Swift and Our Time* (London: Routledge & Kegan Paul, 1973), pp. 9–10

Carole Fabricant on Swift's Excremental Satire

[Carole Fabricant is a professor of English at the University of California at Riverside and the author of *Swift's Landscape* (1982), from which the following extract is taken. Here, Fabricant studies the varying purposes of Swift's use of excrement as a satiric tool in *Gulliver's Travels.*]

Swift explores the excremental realities of rural life in two distinct, indeed antithetical, ways. On the one hand, he stresses their negative association with nastiness, gross physicality, and barbarism; on the other, he suggests their connection with an appealing form of naturalness and spontaneity. The former view is expressed in his depiction of the Yahoos in Part IV of *Gulliver's Travels.* The Houyhnhnm master refers disdainfully to their "strange Disposition to Nastiness and Dirt," one that makes them susceptible to various diseases, which they cure with "a Mixture of *their own Dung* and *Urine,* forcibly put down [their] Throat." In Gulliver's first encounter with them, they "discharge[d] their Excrements on [his] Head," causing him to become "almost stifled with the Filth, which fell about [him] on every Side." Later, "a young Male of three Years old" rebuffed his overtures of tenderness and "voided its filthy Excrements of a yellow liquid Substance, all over [his] Cloaths." Despite the fact that he claims to have discovered a kind of Edenic realm presided over by perfect beings, Gulliver in Houyhnhnmland, like his creator in the Liberties, finds himself in the midst of a dung-filled, stench-ridden environment, forced repeatedly to negotiate his way through the muck and to confront physically repugnant aspects of his surroundings in very immediate ways. He, like Swift, displays a rather unseemly preoccupation with his messy fate and disgustedly lashes out against it—although he, of course, lacks Swift's capacity for dealing both humorously and realistically with similarly unpleasant features of his landscape.

In many ways, the depiction of the Yahoos, as Sir Charles Firth noted, "recalls the description given by Swift, in prose pamphlets written about the same time, of the people whom he terms 'the savage old Irish.'" More broadly, the Yahoos embody characteristics that Swift periodically observed in the Irish people as a whole: slovenliness, squalor, and a certain kind of barbarity, paradoxically coexisting with an excessive submissiveness to authority (the Yahoo leader's favorite would "*lick his Master's Feet and Posteriors*"—not to mention their basic position as a servant class to a ruling elite, who seem to have established a kind of Equestrian Ascendancy. On one level the Yahoos are the Irish as perceived with lofty disdain by a highly cultivated elite who have fully sublimated all biological and emotional urges to higher forms of rational thought and civilized behavior. They are the Irish adjudged by English (hence also Gulliverian) standards as subhuman (or rather, subequestrian) creatures whose excremental activities bespeak an atavistic force that must be kept under tight control—creatures who must be "inclosed," tamed as draught or carriage animals, and consigned to "Huts" perhaps not very different from the notorious Irish "cabbins," finally to be deemed unfit for anything but extermination.

The satire of Part IV cuts both ways, casting a critical light on *both* the brutish, slavish Yahoos and (though less obviously) on their icily detached, colonial masters. Swift was himself at various periods in his life a Yahoo bent on denying his true origins in order to be accepted as a Houyhnhnm before he, like Gulliver, was "exiled" and forced to return to "Yahooland." In this sense, Gulliver in Part IV is the Swift who on occasion repudiated his links to his fellow countrymen, choosing to see the Irish as little better than dabblers in, and devourers of, their own excrement—as wallowers in filthy conditions that were self-generated rather than created by external circumstances.

The point to be stressed in all of this is that the complex, shifting perspectives explored in Gulliver's fourth voyage are inextricably linked to an existing landscape and to its actual inhabitants. Thomas M. Curley maintains that the Yahoos "have much in common with the benighted Australian aborigines of Dampier's New Holland," but I am arguing they have even more in common with the "aborigines" of eighteenth-century Ireland, whom Swift, indeed, on several occasions likened to Laplanders, Hottentots, and other exotic creatures living wild, primitive existences in remote parts of the world. In one instance he avers that "whatever Stranger took such a Journey [through Ireland], would be apt to think himself travelling in *Lapland,* or *Ysland*. . ." Swift's personal travels through the more isolated regions of Ireland gave him firsthand knowledge of the omnipresent squalor, visibly dramatized by the excremental realities, that characterized the Irish countryside. In Part IV of *Gulliver's Travels,* the brutish, dung-filled world of the Irish is treated largely with revulsion and contempt; elsewhere in Swift's writings, this world is treated with alternating pity, anguish, and outrage against the external forces responsible for these conditions.

—Carole Fabricant, *Swift's Landscape* (Baltimore: Johns Hopkins University Press, 1982), pp. 34–36

Patrick Reilly on Gulliver in Lilliput

[Patrick Reilly is the author of *George Orwell: The Age's Adversity* (1986), *The Literature of Guilt: From Gulliver to Golding* (1987), and *Lord of the Flies: Fathers and Sons* (1992). In this extract, taken from his book on Swift, Reilly studies Gulliver's curious position as both a giant and a captive in Lilliput.]

Irony is present from the start in the simultaneous recreation of Gulliver as giant and prisoner. His first impulse to resist as a match for their greatest army is followed by a prudential decision to submit, the linguistic problem circumvented by calling upon the sun as witness of the promise. The Lilliputians evince a similar capacity for prudential morality. They don't try to kill him while he sleeps, sensibly, since the aroused giant would have burst his bonds and caused a blood-bath. The initial relationship between giant and little people is a perfect *exemplum* of Swift's lifelong thesis that decency and commonsense, morality and reason, are ideal bedfellows, that men go to heaven with half the pains of the hellward journey.

The irony of Gulliver's dual status—giant and captive—is, however, soon matched in the ambivalent Lilliputian response. He is, clearly, a notable acquisition; when he eats and drinks, they exhibit an ecstatic proprietary pride in the doer of these wonders. When, freed from the ropes but securely chained, he at last stands erect, they gasp with delighted astonishment. Their attitude to him is rather like Magwitch's to Pip: my gentleman, our giant. But pride competes with other considerations. Like a modern nuclear reactor, Gulliver is both promise and threat, at once source of power and fear, and however gentle and obedient, he poses serious problems for his hosts' technology. What if he breaks loose, runs amok, causes famine or plague? Even if they manage to kill him, will not the stench of the monstrous carcass produce disastrous environmental pollution? Can they afford so costly a luxury with the consequent strain upon their tiny resources?—he needs six hundred domestics and armies of craftsmen of all kinds from joiners to tailors, he consumes daily enough food to keep 1728

Lilliputians alive, the removal of his excreta requires a squad of labourers with wheelbarrows working a full shift.

His everyday acts are potential catastrophes: a man who extinguishes conflagrations simply by urinating might be welcome in London in 1666 or Chicago in 1871, but always there is the fear that he might just as easily drown the government as save the city. His mere presence is a peril in town or country. He must stick to the highways and stay out of the fields where a stroll would mean total devastation. Visiting the metropolis, he has to wear a short coat for fear of destroying buildings and there is a two hours' curfew to avoid a massacre of citizens. What if he sleepwalks? or sneezes? It's like living with a petro-chemical complex on the doorstep. Every time he relieves himself, the health authorities face a major crisis in pollution disposal, the modern equivalent of a giant oil tanker wrecked daily on your coast. When he eats and drinks the spectacle is magnificent, but pride in his prowess and aesthetic delight are tempered by a frightened glance at the ravaged foodstore or the ledgers of a desperate exchequer. And yet the Lilliputians clearly find it a comfort to have a giant on their side and the high risks of his maintenance nag less when he puts on a fearsome display of the latest European weaponry; waving his scimitar or firing his pistols, he appeals to the same emotions, brings the same comforting reassurance, as do the newest NATO missiles or the massive Warsaw Pact armaments rolling through Red Square.

From the start he decides to be a 'good' giant, earn his parole by contradicting the stereotype of the wicked ogre. His first conscious impersonation is of a mock Polyphemus. When the hooligans who stone him are delivered to him by the military for punishment, he puts them in his pocket and takes one out, like the Cyclops with the companions of Ulysses, as though he were about to eat him. The officers' dismay gives way to rejoicing when instead he uses his terrible knife to cut the culprits' bonds before gently setting them free—the ogre is really a genial giant, forever obliging and anxious not to disturb. He passes with full marks this clemency test and in a remarkable demonstration of power and magnanimity completely fulfills Isabella's injunction to the great ones of the world:

> O, 'tis excellent
> To have a giant's strength, but it is tyrannous
> To use it like a giant.

The policy of being a model prisoner seems to pay off when the Emperor, hearing of the incident, decides to give Gulliver a chance to prove himself 'a useful servant'. He becomes a kind of court entertainer or circus strong-man, a Samson desperately eager to placate his captors by feats of strength and entertainments, using his handkerchief as exercise ground for the royal cavalry, straddling his legs to provide an imposing triumphal arch for the full military parade. Mildness reaches a charming apogee as the natives dance in his hand and the children play hide-and-seek in his hair—there could be no more striking proof that the passage from Polyphemus to lovable giant has been fully accomplished.
—Patrick Reilly, *Jonathan Swift: The Brave Desponder* (Carbondale: Southern Illinois University Press, 1982), pp. 178–80

Irvin Ehrenpreis on the Autobiographical Significance of *Gulliver's Travels*

[Irvin Ehrenpreis (1920–1985) was among the leading scholars of Swift and of eighteenth-century literature in general. Among his works are *The Personality of Swift* (1958), *Acts of Implication* (1980), and a landmark three-volume biography of Swift, *Swift: The Man, His Works, and the Age* (1962–83), from which the following extract is taken. Here, Ehrenpreis interprets the various sections of *Gulliver's Travels* as reflecting different facets of Swift's previous life.]

The rhythm of the four parts of *Gulliver* suggests stages in Swift's memories. In its historical allusions, Part One points mainly to the public events of the years 1708–15. The dispelling of Gulliver's illusions as he learns more and more about the imperial court evokes the enlightenment Swift suffered during the years 1711–14. Part Two, I suspect, reverts to the private events of the years 1688–99. The giant king and his wife have touches of Temple and Dorothy Osborne. Glumdalclitch—who leaves her family to join Gulliver, and whom he then deserts—has touches of Esther Johnson; and so has the queen (whose 'weak stomach' is like Stella's). Part Three, the least coherent, alludes to the public events of the years 1715–25. The material is not yet digested; the narrative is fragmentary. Part Four, I speculate, alludes quite unconsciously to Swift's childhood and youth, suggesting an early lack of self-respect, of hostility toward adults, and fear of sexuality. So Swift assigns the Houyhnhnms to a remarkably primitive culture, lacking metals and the wheel. They exist in the pastoral, Saturnian myth of an innocence preceding civilization and associated with childhood.

The design of *Gulliver* also shows the effects of Swift's travels and of his fondness for travel books. The ease and regularity with which Gulliver leaves his wife and children correspond to Swift's habit of abandoning Stella. Swift's voyages between England and Ireland were, for him, like shuttlings between civilization and barbarism. When he travelled within Ireland, he seemed often to navigate seas of bestiality in order to reach islets of human culture; and the sharpness of the contrasts gave him a point of view for his comic, ironic survey of mankind.

—Irvin Ehrenpreis, *Swift: The Man, His Works, and the Age* (Cambridge, MA: Harvard University Press, 1983), Vol. 3, pp. 457–58

Nigel Wood on Gulliver as Artist

[Nigel Wood is the coeditor of *John Gay and the Scriblerus Club* (1989) and the author of *Swift* (1986), from which the following extract is taken. Here, Wood maintains that, in spite of his protestations to recording the unvarnished truth, Gulliver is in fact a literary artist whose account contains subtleties, complexities, and contradictions.]

Gulliver's 'Truth' is rarely a moral quality. Frequently, he will assure us of his veracity but this is usually in relation to the details of his narrative and not to any universal grasp of ethical problems. He does not refrain from including examples of micturation (such as extinguishing the fire at the Lilliputian Empress' apartment or even defecation). Yet, especially in Lilliput, he often suggests a reality exterior to his own abbreviated discourse, not troubling the reader with the minutiae of superfluous description. In Brobdingnag, where the physical threat is more immediate, he rarely spends as much time on providing plausible credentials for his own narrative.

There is one passage, however, where Gulliver begs the 'gentle Reader' for forbearance and, in so doing, suggests a change in tone. After Gulliver's frantic and almost heroic struggle with the monstrous rats on his mistress' bed, an unusually limpid narration of actions rather than state of mind or observations on alien cultures, he apologises for dwelling on his discharging of 'the Necessities of Nature' after it. However, the preceding narrative has surely undercut such precious solicitude for the reader. Gulliver-as-actor has surely excused any unartful story-telling by Gulliver-as-teller. To protest this much is fatuous and, what is more, alerts the reader to the weak sides in his text, especially as to its usefulness. The 'Necessities of Nature' are described, 'however insignificant they may appear to grovelling vulgar Minds', in order to allow philosophers to 'enlarge [their] Thoughts and Imagination, and apply them to the Benefit of publick as well as private Life'. The opposite is truer to the experience of reading *Gulliver*, for such redundancy of detail has no such expansive effect. Gulliver, 'chiefly studious of Truth', cannot deduce from his own experiences any 'complex ideas' of either ethical or aesthetic value. His claim to dispense with 'any Ornaments of Learning, or of Style' promise almost total recall, deflected by the minimum of artifice. Indeed, the sojourn in Brobdingnag 'made so strong an Impression on [his] Mind, and is so deeply fixed in [his] Memory, that in Committing it to Paper, [he] did not omit one material Circumstance'. The very next sentence erases this faithfulness to experience completely: 'However, upon a strict Review, I blotted out several Passages of less Moment which were in my first Copy, for fear of being censured as tedious and trifling, whereof Travellers are often, perhaps not without Justice, accused'. Gulliver is, after all, an artist. The reader cannot receive the unvarnished 'truth' of his first draft at all. We acknowledge the same sense of erasure if we turn to the Prefaces of *Robinson Crusoe* or *Moll Flanders* (1722) after reading the main text. For *Crusoe* we discover that the aim of the whole has not been to mirror the serendipitous events of his travels but 'to justify and honour the Wisdom of Providence in all the Variety of our Circumstances, let them happen how they will'. Whilst there is no 'Appearance of Fiction' in the tale and it provides 'a just History of Fact', this is in turn affirmed by the 'Editor'. Moll does not write her own preface either, but rather her amanuensis who has 'put it into a dress fit to be seen, and to make it speak language fit to be read'—not the accents of Newgate prison.

—Nigel Wood, *Swift* (Atlantic Highlands, NJ: Humanities Press, 1986), pp. 71–73

PAUL K. ALKON ON *GULLIVER'S TRAVELS* AS A FORERUNNER OF SCIENCE FICTION

[Paul K. Alkon, a professor of English at the University of Southern California, has written *The Origins of Futuristic Fiction* (1987) and *Science Fiction Before 1900* (1994). In this extract, Alkon sees *Gulliver's Travels* as a significant forerunner to science fiction in its utilization of the imaginary voyage, utopia and anti-utopia, and satire on society.]

What I have for convenience called the old wave view of science fiction is concerned primarily with how it holds a mirror up to present or possible future reality, whether social or scientific, and with each author's explicit rhetorical purposes for doing so. Genre is defined narrowly in terms of subject matter in relationship to scientific concepts. The boundary between science fiction and other genres is clear. From this perspective the voyages to Lilliput and Brobdingnag are adventure-fantasy, no matter how much they may be inspired by the microscope and telescope. Gulliver's third voyage is science fiction, but only while he is on the Flying Island, in Lagado, and among the Struldbruggs. The fourth voyage is a variety of utopia. *Gulliver's Travels* as a whole lacks generic unity but is no worse for that. Insofar as it is science fiction it is deplorable for the very cleverness of its attack on science, but no more deplorable than any other kind of antiscientific rhetoric. Swift gets credit for being the first English writer of true science fiction but is reprehensible for his hostility to science and his lack of faith in the idea of progress. Partly on account of taking these negative attitudes as a rhetorical stance, the third voyage, despite its virtues as pioneering science fiction, seems the weakest. Swift remains the foremost English satirist, but *Gulliver's Travels* is relegated to the remote past of science fiction.

For new wave theorists of science fiction Swift is our contemporary. The *Travels* is our great model. The eighteenth century is in dialogic relationship to the twentieth century. All the heroes of science fiction are more or less striking analogues of Lemuel Gulliver. The genre is defined in terms of how it affects the reader's perception of reality, and any technique or subject matter that can bring about cognitive estrangement is legitimate. There are fluid, not rigid boundaries between other genres and science fiction. It may as properly be used to attack as to defend science. *Gulliver's Travels* becomes a unified work with all of its components—imaginary voyage, utopia, antiutopia, fantasy, and satire—subordinated as parts of a coherent whole, because amid their other purposes they all help sustain cognitive estrangement. Other effects may predominate locally. But the *Travels* moves through varying degrees of strangeness and corresponding arousal of cognitive estrangement to an appropriate climax (not simply to a conundrum for critics) in the fourth part. Gulliver's last voyage, rather than part 3, becomes the most powerful science fiction in the *Travels* because, of all the creatures Gulliver encounters, the

Houyhnhynms are the most genuinely alien—the most shockingly different.

Neither in their shape, their mentality, nor their social forms do they recall humans, that is to say, our world—as do the Lilliputians, Brobdingnagians, and even the mad scientists of Laputa and Lagado. The Houyhnhynms are truly *other*. Their appearance, their well-ordered society, their honesty, and above all, of course, their very ability to love or hate as we do drives Gulliver mad—and too often drives critics the same direction by their endless dispute over Swift's intentions. When the *Travels* are seen in the light of recent science fiction, however, there is no need to enter that hopeless debate. Rather than asking the unanswerable question of whether Swift intended readers to accept the Houyhnhynms as Gulliver does for a model in all things, we may take the evident difficulty of doing so as a measure of Swift's success in making readers look at humanity from a radically estranged perspective; that perspective forces any thinking person to assess the springs of human behavior instead of just taking note of the myriad forms of human folly satirized *en route* to Gulliver's final lodging in the stable. Heightened awareness, by means of contrast with the Houyhnhynms, of what we *are* rather than the pinpointing of an explicit proposal from Swift (via their nature or some combination of theirs and ours) of what to do about it, can be taken as a satisfactory outcome of reading the *Travels*. There have certainly been other critical routes to this conclusion. I do not propose it as an exclusive advantage of taking *Gulliver's Travels* as science fiction. But I suggest that by doing so we can nicely specify not merely the targets of its satire but the effects of its satire upon readers. We can also define its social role in relationship to its aesthetic virtues, which are in fact also the virtues of our best science fiction.

—Paul K. Alkon, "*Gulliver* and the Origins of Science Fiction," *The Genres of* Gulliver's Travels, ed. Frederik N. Smith (Newark: University of Delaware Press, 1990), pp. 174–76

DENNIS TODD ON GULLIVER'S DISSOLUTION OF IDENTITY

[Dennis Todd is a professor of English at Georgetown University. In this extract, Todd believes that the various personas that Lemuel Gulliver adopts throughout *Gulliver's Travels* cause his personality to dissolve toward the end of the book.]

On the basis of this expectation, Swift leads us to assume larger integrities of character, for out of the voice of Gulliver, Swift is always precipitating intimations of a coherence. The voice of Gulliver keeps falling into well-known literary types or roles or characters (in the Theophrastan sense) or broad social stereotypes, all of which recur repeatedly and consistently throughout the work: Gulliver the "prostitute Flatterer"; Gulliver the patriot, who "perpetually dins our ears with Praises of his Country, in the midst of Corruptions"; Gulliver the latter-day Timon, the foolish ingenue betrayed by his own susceptibility to flattery into misanthropy; Gulliver the stolid middle-class Englishman; Gulliver the satiric surgeon, the critical observer and anatomist of man's ills; Gulliver the satirist satirized; Gulliver the court fool; the Gulliver who is gulled by others; the Gulliver who gulls himself. Not only do these roles and types tease us with the promise of at least some coherence and stability, but they often slide neatly into each other to intimate a more complex, layered self (i.e., Gulliver's role as a middle-class Englishman gives a concrete social and psychological context to his literary role as the foolish ingenue, and together they suggest a set of plausible, concrete motives for his bedazzlement at foreign courts and his becoming the flatterer). And often Swift creates chains of situations that imply a sustained continuity of feeling, attitude, and motive (i.e., the extraordinary care Swift takes to lead up to Gulliver's offer of gunpowder). And often these roles and types and situations dovetail across the whole expanse of the book, creating such complexities of character as I have argued for in explaining Gulliver's playing the monster. In short, Swift encourages us to *think of* Gulliver as a character, to expect to hear in his voice the lines of a coherent selfhood. And then, having half fulfilled this expectation, Swift half defeats it. Because of their typicality and literariness, we are always aware that these roles are just roles, and though often they slide together into coherency, they just as often rub against each other, create unresolvable contradictions, become unstable, and collapse into incoherency. The effect of Swift's play with the discontinuities *and* continuities of voice is to create in us as we are reading a sense of a self in Gulliver, but a jerry-built self, one continually constructing itself and continually losing its coherence, dissolving, its identity slipping away before our eyes.

This effect, of course, is similar to the effect created by the Modern Author of *Tale of a Tub.* There, too, we hear an ever-shifting voice, a voice that continually controverts itself, pulled this way and that by the motion and countermotion of ideas, emotions, and intentions at cross-purposes with themselves, spinning apart in its contradictions and instabilities, often at the edge (and often over the edge) of coherence, a voice of a self in the perpetual process of dissolving under the pressures of its own centrifugal energies.

I wanted to call attention to this resemblance because I think that Swift returns in *Gulliver* to his grand theme in the *Tale,* the dissolution of identity, and that in both works he traces this dissolution to the same source. The Modern Author of the *Tale* is always fragmenting himself because he is always articulating himself at the leading edge of the present moment, often clause by clause, driven by the "great Design of an everlasting Remembrance, and never-dying Fame." He must play to the ever-shifting and ever-contradictory expectations of the modern audience, thrusting himself forward in an ever-present now in order to dominate them and shape their opinion of him, making a spectacle of himself to establish his superiority, abandoning any continuity or durability of self-identity for the sake of the immediacy of effect. Consequently, his identity becomes "eternally momentary." And this is precisely Gulliver's motive and fate. Gulliver bobs and wheels through poses and attitudes, performing for his various audiences, driven, like the Modern Author of the *Tale,* by an insistent self-assertion, a desire to distinguish himself. Because his audience (both in his head and in the lands he visits) is always changing and always variegated, he too must play to them in a kind of eternal present, constantly shifting stances, feelings, beliefs, and standards, constantly reformulating an identity to suit the context of whatever monstrous world or monstrous moment he happens to find himself in. In the *Tale,* the dissolution of the Modern's identity is figured in that work's central symbol: the Modern Author becomes a tub, all surface surrounding an empty space. In *Gulliver,* Gulliver's dispersion of identity is figured in what I have argued is that work's central symbol: Gulliver becomes a monster, dissolving into the shapeless, incoherent gestures of the ego's desire to distinguish itself.

>—Dennis Todd, "The Hairy Maid at the Harpsichord: Some Speculations on the Meaning of *Gulliver's Travels,*" *Texas Studies in Literature and Language* 34, No. 2 (Summer 1992): 270–71

IAN HIGGINS ON THE POLITICS OF *GULLIVER'S TRAVELS*

> [Ian Higgins is Lecturer in English at the Australian National University in Canberra and author of *Francis Ponge* (1979) and *Swift's Politics* (1994), from which the following extract is taken. Here, Higgins studies some aspects of the political satire in *Gulliver's Travels;* in particular, he sees part three as presenting a searching criticism of the reign of the Hanovers beginning with George I in 1714, which succeeded the reign of the Stuarts (1603–1714). Swift, as a "Jacobite" (a supporter of the Stuart reign), may be suggesting that the Hanover dynasty is a political disaster.]

In Part III of *Gulliver's Travels* there is an arresting possibility that the satirist is suggesting that the settlement of the crown in the House of Hanover has been a political, social and economic catastrophe. There are sufficient 'hints' enabling readers to associate Laputa, the '*Flying* or *Floating Island*', with contemporary Britain and George I's Whig Court. For example, the King and Court are preoccupied to distraction with abstract speculations upon the subjects of 'Mathematicks and Musick'.

George I approved and patronised mathematicians and musicians, and music was the 'reigning Amusement' in London, Gay told Swift in 1723. Like Gulliver's countrymen, the people of Laputa display a 'strong Disposition . . . towards News and Politicks . . . passionately disputing every Inch of a Party Opinion'. The King of Laputa 'would be the most absolute Prince' but his ministers, it seems, are landed men with estates to protect and they 'would never consent to the enslaving their Country'. This King is 'distinguished above all his Predecessors for his Hospitality to Strangers'. There are a considerable number of 'Strangers' from the continent attending at Court. Arraignment of George I for absolutism and for being a foreigner, hostility to Hanoverian 'Strangers', and appeals for a free parliament of landed men to defend the '*Liberties of* England' against a Hanoverian court alleged to be for '*Absolute Power, and Enslaving* the Nation' are topoi in Jacobite Tory pamphleteering of the 1710s and 1720s. Swift's satire specifically alludes to the Hanoverian government's repeal of the provision in the Act of Settlement (1701) forbidding the King to leave England without parliamentary permission. Gulliver reports: 'BY a fundamental Law of this Realm, neither the King nor either of his two elder Sons, are permitted to leave the Island; nor the Queen till she is past Child-bearing'. The passage is not without libellous innuendo. This line of satiric attack also has Jacobite analogues. Jacobite pamphleteers were saying that George I had violated the legislative contract or settlement upon which his right to rule was founded.⟨. . .⟩

Swift may, in fact, encode in Part III disaffection with the Act of Settlement itself by which the Hanoverian dynasty ruled. During Gulliver's stay with that disaffected conservative Lord Munodi he is desired to observe a distant 'ruined Building upon the Side of a Mountain'. Munodi tells Gulliver

> That he had a very convenient Mill within Half a Mile of his House, turned by a Current from a large River, and sufficient for his own Family as well as a great Number of his Tenants. That, about seven Years ago, a Club of those Projectors came to him with Proposals to destroy this Mill, and build another on the Side of that Mountain . . . that being then not very well with the Court, and pressed by many of his Friends, he complied with the Proposal.

The Laputan 'Experiment' miscarried and the result was ruin. The Mill episode has been thought to refer to the disastrous South Sea scheme and to the contemporary mania for entrepreneurial projects. Pat Rogers suggests that it 'is likely that Swift has a subsidiary political point: undesirable innovations include the kind of notions imported when the English leaders went across to Holland to invite over William of Orange'. Contesting received allegorical interpretation of the episode. F. P. Lock nevertheless observes appositely that the 'design of the new mill replacing the old is a better type of an attempt to replace one dynasty with another than it is of a trading and financial concern'. In line with his thesis, Lock does not propose this as 'a serious interpretation' but as an example of how easily allegorical readings can be generated in criticism. But what if a Jacobitical dynastic critique is obliquely present in the text? The consequence should be a major revision of our understanding of the politics of the text and its author. Munodi, out of favour with the Court, complied with this project 'about seven Years ago' (i.e. c. 1701). In 1701, the Tories, out of favour with William III, complied with the alteration of the hereditary succession in the Act of Settlement, the Act being framed with significant limitations restricting the power of future monarchs (see *PW*, VIII, 94 for Swift's witness of Tory framing of the Settlement in 1701). Gulliver tells us that 'I had my self been a Sort of Projector in my younger Days'. As the *Discourse of the Contests and Dissentions* indicates, Swift had been (at least nominally) a Whig in 1701. The fact that in contemporary political iconography a windmill was associated with the Pretender might have enabled a Tory dynastic reading of the Mill episode in Swift's text: the destruction of the succession in the hereditary House of Stuart in 1701 and radical deviation to the distant House of Hanover with ruinous consequences.

—Ian Higgins, *Swift's Politics: a Study in Disaffection*
(Cambridge: Cambridge University Press, 1994), pp. 176–79

Books by Jonathan Swift

A Discourse of the Contests and Dissensions between the Nobles and the Commons in Athens and Rome. 1701.

A Tale of a Tub, Written for the Universal Improvement of Mankind; to Which Is Added an Account of a Battel between the Antient and Modern Books in St. James's Library. 1704.

Predictions for the Year 1708, by Isaac Bickerstaff Esq. 1708.

The Accomplishment of the First of Mr. Bickerstaff's Predictions: Being an Account of the Death of Mr. Partrige. 1708.

An Elegy on Mr. Partrige, the Almanack-Maker. 1708.

A Vindication of Isaac Bickerstaff Esq. 1709.

A Letter from a Member of the House of Commons in Ireland to a Member of the House of Commons in England, concerning the Sacramental Test. 1709.

Baucis and Philemon, Imitated from Ovid. 1709.

A Meditation upon a Broom-Stick. 1710.

An Apology for the Tale of a Tub. 1711.

Miscellanies in Prose and Verse. 1711.

The Conduct of the Allies. 1711.

The Fable of Midas. 1712.

A Proposal for Correcting, Improving, and Ascertaining the English Tongue. 1712.

Part of the Seventh Epistle of the First Book of Horace Imitated. 1713.

The Importance of the Guardian Considered. 1713.

The First Ode of the Second Book of Horace Paraphras'd. 1714.

The Publick Spirit of the Whigs. 1714.

A Proposal for the Universal Use of Irish Manufacture. 1720.

Miscellaneous Works Comical and Diverting. 1720.

The Present Miserable State of Ireland. 1721.

A Letter to the Shop-Keepers, Tradesmen, Farmers, and Common People of Ireland, concerning the Brass Half-Pence Coined by Mr. Woods, by M. B. Drapier. 1724.

A Letter to Mr. Harding the Printer, by M. B. Drapier. 1724.

Fraud Detected; or, The Hibernian Patriot [*The Drapier's Letters*]. 1725.

Cadenus and Vanessa. 1726.

Travels into Several Remote Nations of the World, in Four Parts, by Lemuel Gulliver, First a Surgeon, and Then a Captain of Several Ships [*Gulliver's Travels*]. 1726. 2 vols.

Miscellanies in Prose and Verse (with Alexander Pope, John Arbuthnot et al.). 1727 (Volumes 1–3); 1732 (Volume 4); 1735 (Volume 5).

A Short View of the State of Ireland. 1728.

The Intelligencer (with Thomas Sheridan). 1728. 20 nos.

The Journal of a Dublin Lady. 1729.

A Modest Proposal for Preventing the Children of Poor People from Being a Burthen to Their Parents, or the Country, and for Making Them Beneficial to the Publick. 1729.

An Epistle to His Excellency John Lord Carteret, Lord Lieutenant of Ireland. 1730.

A Libel on D—— D———— and a Certain Great Lord. 1730.

A Panegyric on the Reverend D—n S———t. 1730.

To Doctor D–L—Y, on the Libels Writ against Him. 1730.

An Answer to Dr. D——y's Fable of the Pheasant and the Lark. 1730.

A Proposal Humbly Offer'd to the P————t, for the More Effectual Preventing the Further Growth of Popery. 1731.

The Lady's Dressing Room; to Which Is Added a Poem on Cutting Down the Old Thorn at Market Hill. 1732.

The Advantages Propos'd by Repealing the Sacramental, Impartially Considered. 1732.

The Life and Genuine Character of Doctor Swift. 1733.

The Drapier's Miscellany. 1733.

On Poetry: A Rhapsody. 1733.

Works. 1735. 4 vols.

The Furniture of a Woman's Mind. c. 1735.

Poetical Works. 1736.

Works. 1738. 6 vols.

Political Tracts. 1738. 2 vols.

An Imitation of the Sixth Satire of the Second Book of Horace. 1738.

A Complete Collection of Genteel and Ingenious Conversation, According to the Most Polite Mode and Method Now Used at Court, and in the Best Companies of England, in Three Dialogues. 1738.

Verses on the Death of Doctor Swift. 1739.

Some Free Thoughts upon the Present State of Affairs, Written in the Year 1714. 1741.{?}

Letters to and from Dr. Jonathan Swift from the Year 1714 to 1737. 1741.

Directions to Servants. 1745.

Works. 1746. 8 vols.

Works. 1751. 14 vols.

Works. Ed. John Hawkesworth. 1755. 12 vols.

Letters Written by the Late Jonathan Swift, D.D., and Several of His Friends. Ed. John Hawkesworth and Deane Swift. 1768–69. 6 vols.

Poetical Works. 1778. 4 vols.

Works. Ed. Thomas Sheridan. 1784. 17 vols.

Works. Ed. Sir Walter Scott. 1814. 19 vols.

Prose Works. Ed. Temple Scott. 1898–1909. 12 vols.

The Journal to Stella. Ed. George A. Aitken. 1901.

Correspondence. Ed. F. Erlington Ball. 1910–14. 6 vols.

Vanessa and Her Correspondence with Swift. Ed. A. M. Freeman. 1921.

Letters to Charles Ford. Ed. David Nichol Smith. 1935.

Poems. Ed. Harold Williams. 1937. 3 vols.

Prose Works. Ed. Herbert Davis. 1939–68. 14 vols.

The Journal to Stella. Ed. Harold Williams. 1948. 2 vols.

Correspondence. Ed. Harold Williams. 1963–65. 5 vols.

Complete Poems. Ed. Pat Rogers. 1983.

Account Books. Ed. Paul V. Thompson and Dorothy Jay Thompson. 1984.

Swift's Irish Pamphlets: An Introductory Selection. Ed. Joseph McMinn. 1991.

Works about Jonathan Swift and *Gulliver's Travels*

Bellamy, Liz. *Jonathan Swift's* Gulliver's Travels. New York: St. Martin's Press, 1992.

Bentman, Raymond. "Satiric Structure and Tone in the Conclusion of *Gulliver's Travels*." *Studies in English Literature 1500–1900* 11 (1971): 535–48.

Bloom, Harold, ed. *Jonathan Swift*. New York: Chelsea House, 1986.

———, ed. *Jonathan Swift's* Gulliver's Travels. New York: Chelsea House, 1986.

Carnochan, W. B. *Lemuel Gulliver's Mirror for Man*. Berkeley: University of California Press, 1968.

Case, Arthur E. *Four Essays on* Gulliver's Travels. Princeton: Princeton University Press, 1945.

Castle, Terry J. "Why the Houyhnhnms Don't Write: Swift, Satire and the Fear of the Text." *Essays in Literature* 7 (1980): 31–44.

Champion, Larry S. "Gulliver's Voyages: The Framing Events as a Guide to Interpretation." *Texas Studies in Literature and Language* 10 (1969): 529–36.

Donoghue, Denis. *Jonathan Swift: A Critical Introduction*. Cambridge: Cambridge University Press, 1969.

Downie, J. A. *Jonathan Swift, Political Writer*. London: Routledge & Kegan Paul, 1984.

Erskine-Hill, Howard. *Jonathan Swift:* Gulliver's Travels. Cambridge: Cambridge University Press, 1993.

Ewald, William B. *The Masks of Jonathan Swift*. Cambridge, MA: Harvard University Press, 1954.

Ferguson, Oliver Watkins. *Jonathan Swift, Giant in Chains*. New York: Liveright, 1940.

Francus, Marilyn. *The Converting Imagination: Linguistic Theory and Swift's Satiric Prose.* Carbondale: Southern Illinois University Press, 1994.

Gilbert, Jack G. *Jonathan Swift: Romantic and Cynic Moralist.* Austin: University of Texas Press, 1966.

Gill, James E. "Beast over Man: Theriophilic Paradox in Gulliver's 'Voyage to the Country of the Houyhnhnms.'" *Studies in Philology* 67 (1970): 532–49.

Gravil, Richard, ed. *Swift:* Gulliver's Travels: *A Casebook.* London: Macmillan, 1974.

Guilhamet, Leon. *Swift and the Transformation of Genre.* Philadelphia: University of Pennsylvania Press, 1987.

Hinnant, Charles H. *Purity and Defilement in* Gulliver's Travels. New York: St. Martin's Press, 1977.

Holly, Grant. "Travel and Translation: Textuality in *Gulliver's Travels.*" *Criticism* 21 (1979): 134–52.

Jeffares, A. Norman, ed. *Swift: Modern Judgements.* London: Macmillan, 1969.

Kelly, Ann Cline. *Swift and the English Language.* Philadelphia: University of Pennsylvania Press, 1988.

Landa, Louis A. *Swift and the Church of Ireland.* Oxford: Clarendon Press, 1954.

Lee, Jae Num. *Swift and Scatalogical Satire.* Albuquerque: University of New Mexico Press, 1971.

Lock, F. P. *The Politics of* Gulliver's Travels. Oxford: Clarendon Press, 1980.

McManmon, John J. "The Problem of a Religious Interpretation of Gulliver's Fourth Voyage." *Journal of the History of Ideas* 27 (1966): 59–72.

Mezciems, Jenny. "The Unity of Swift's 'Voyage to Laputa': Structure as Meaning in Utopian Fiction." *Modern Language Review* 72 (1977): 1–21.

Murry, John Middleton. *Jonathan Swift: A Critical Biography.* London: Jonathan Cape, 1954.

Nokes, David. *Jonathan Swift, a Hypocrite Reversed: A Critical Biography.* Oxford: Oxford University Press, 1985.

Orwell, George. "Politics vs. Literature: An Examination of *Gulliver's Travels.*" In *The Collected Essays, Journalism and Letters of George Orwell.* Ed. Sonia Orwell and Ian Angus. New York: Harcourt, Brace & World, 1968, Vol. 4, pp. 205–23.

Paulson, Ronald. *The Fictions of Satire.* Baltimore: Johns Hopkins University Press, 1967.

Philmus, Robert M. "Swift and the Question of Allegory: The Case of *Gulliver's Travels.*" *English Studies in Canada* 18 (1992): 157–79.

Price, Martin. *Swift's Rhetorical Art.* New Haven: Yale University Press, 1953.

———. *To the Palace of Wisdom: Studies in Order and Energy from Dryden to Blake.* Carbondale: Southern Illinois University Press, 1964.

Probyn, Clive T. *The Art of Jonathan Swift.* London: Vision Press, 1978.

———, ed. *Jonathan Swift: The Contemporary Background.* Manchester, UK: Manchester University Press, 1978.

Quinlan, Maurice. "Swift's Use of Literalization as a Rhetorical Device." *PMLA* 82 (1967): 516–21.

Rawson, Claude, ed. *The Character of Swift's Satire: A Revised Focus.* Newark: University of Delaware Press, 1983.

Rodino, Richard H. " 'Splendide Mendax': Authors, Characters, and Readers in *Gulliver's Travels.*" *PMLA* 106 (1991): 1054–70.

Rosenheim, E. W. *Swift and the Satirist's Art.* Chicago: University of Chicago Press, 1963.

Steele, Peter. *Jonathan Swift: Preacher and Jester.* Oxford: Oxford University Press, 1978.

Suits, Conrad. "The Role of Horses in 'A Voyage to the Houyhnhnms.' " *University of Toronto Quarterly* 34 (1964–65): 118–32.

Vickers, Brian, ed. *The World of Jonathan Swift: Essays for the Tercentenary*. Cambridge, MA: Harvard University Press, 1968.

Zimmerman, Everett. *Swift's Narrative Satires: Author and Authority*. Ithaca, NY: Cornell University Press, 1983.

Index of Themes and Ideas

ACT OF SETTLEMENT (1701), as subject of satire, 64–65

BALNIBARBI, and its role in the book, 18, 19, 43

BIG-ENDIANS, and their role in the book, 13

BLEFUSCU, and its role in the book, 11, 13–14, 30

BROBDINGNAG: Gulliver deemed a *lusus naturae* in, 16; Gulliver sexually abused in, 17, 43; Gulliver snatched by a bird in, 18; Gulliver's shame in, 15; monkey in, 17; Orwell on, 41–42; and its role in the book, 15–18, 32, 34–35, 43, 45, 57–58, 59, 60; six-foot breast in, 15

DISCOURSES OF THE CONTESTS AND DISSENTIONS, and how it compares, 65

DISSOLUTION OF IDENTITY, as theme, 61–63

EDUCATION, as subject of satire, 19, 38–39

ENGLAND: Gulliver's final return to, 23; and Gulliver's patriotism, 16, 17, 20, 24, 40, 48; Ireland vs., 56; satire of court-life in, 12–13, 43, 55–56; satire of government in, 16, 20, 24, 41–42, 63–65

EXCREMENT, as symbol, 12, 15, 21, 50–52, 57

GLUBBDUBDRIB, and its role in the book, 18, 20

GLUMDALCLITCH, and her role in the book, 15–16, 17, 30–31, 43, 56

GODWIN, WILLIAM, Swift compared to, 33

GRAND ACADEMY, and its role in the book, 19–20

GULLIVER, LEMUEL: as artist, 56–58; blindness of, 5–6, 11; contradictions in character of, 6, 40, 46–48, 61–63; disillusionment of, 23, 40, 60; insanity of, 5; as literal-minded, 5–6; misanthropy of, 40, 46–48, 60; as monster, 61–63; naivete of, 34–35, 40, 46–48; as satirist, 46–48, 61; Swift's relation to, 5, 11, 14, 19, 32, 46–48, 51, 52; as sympathetic, 6; veracity of, 14, 21–22, 23, 48, 57–58

GULLIVER'S TRAVELS: autobiographical significance of, 34, 55–56, 65; bewilderment in, 48–50, 59; as children's book, 5, 10, 35–37; as comedy of incomprehension, 6; as comic masterpiece, 42–44; composition of, 38; contemporary reactions to, 26–27; emotional intensity of, 36–37; as forerunner of science fiction, 58–60; Gay on, 26–27; Hazlitt on moral lessons of, 29–31; as impious, 27; irony of, 36–37, 40, 44–46, 50, 53; Johnson's aversion to, 5; misanthropy of, 26–31, 41, 42–44, 45; opening of, 48; publication of, 10; Raleigh on, 34–35; reader's response to, 12, 48–50, 57–58, 62; realism in, 34–35, 36, 37; role of women in, 15, 17, 18–19, 27, 56; savage quality of, 5, 35; Scott on, 28–29; sexuality in, 17, 38–39, 43, 56; shifting points of view in, 40, 47–50, 51–52; structure of, 44–46, 56, 59; Swift's purpose in, 5–7, 11, 25–27, 30–31, 35, 42–46, 60

HISTORY, as subject of satire, 20

HOUYHNHNMS: as alien, 59–60; and desire to exterminate the Yahoos, 7; as devoid of imagination, 6, 22; as distopian society, 59–60; Gulliver adopts perspective of, 5, 21, 40, 60; Gulliver's attempts to bribe, 21; reason employed by, 5, 6, 21–23; 43–44; speech of, 21–22; Swift's relation to, 6–7, 55–56, 60; as utopian society, 22, 33, 44, 51, 56, 59; "Voyage to Laputa" in relation to, 45–46

HUMAN NATURE, as theme, 24, 26–31, 44, 45, 59–60

INFERNO (Dante), and how it compares, 33–34

IRELAND, as subject of satire, 51–52, 56

JAPAN, and its role in the book, 18, 20

LAGADO, and its role in the book, 19–20, 59, 60

LAPUTA: and George I, 63–65; Mill episode on, 64–65; and its role in the book, 5, 18–19, 43, 60; as untidy and superficial episode, 45–46; women of, 18–19

LILLIPUT: criminal code in, 38; educational system in, 38–39; fire doused by Gulliver's urine in, 14, 54, 57; Gulliver as prisoner in, 11, 53–55; principles of government in, 38, 48; and its role in the book, 5, 11–15, 34–35, 45; as utopia, 37–39

LITTLE-ENDIANS, and their role in the book, 13

LUGGNAGG, and its role in the book, 18, 20, 22

MODEST PROPOSAL, A, and how it compares, 45

MOLL FLANDERS (Defoe), and how it compares, 58

MUNODI, LORD, and his role in the book, 64–65

OLD AGE, as theme, 20, 22, 34

PEDRO, DON, and his role in the book, 23

PERSPECTIVE, as theme, 11–17, 23, 24, 32, 60

PHYSICAL VS. INTELLECTUAL, as theme, 6, 18–19, 21–22; 28–29; 38–39, 50–52, 57–58

POLITICS, as subject of satire, 10, 12–14, 16, 20, 35, 36, 43, 45, 55–56, 63–65

REASON, as theme, 5–7, 13, 18–19, 21–22; 43–44; 48, 56–58

ROBINSON CRUSOE (Defoe), and how it compares, 36, 58

ROYAL SOCIETY, as subject of satire, 19

SCIENCE, as subject of satire, 12, 17, 18–20, 43, 45, 59

SELF-KNOWLEDGE, as theme, 5–6, 30–31, 43–44

SLAMECKSANS, and their role in the book, 13

STRULDBRUGGS, and their role in the book, 20, 22, 34

SWIFT, JONATHAN: declared insane, 5, 10, 43; education of, 8; in Ireland, 9, 56; life of, 8–10; as member of the Scriblerus Club, 9, 26; misanthropy of, 10, 25–26, 29–32, 33; on money, 32; old age feared by, 34; self-hatred of, 31–32; as Tory, 9, 31, 64–65

SYMPSON, MR., and his role in the book, 11, 46, 49

TALE OF THE TUB, A, and how it compares, 45, 46, 62–63

TRAMECKSANS, and their role in the book, 13

TRAVEL BOOKS, as subject of satire, 10, 11, 35–37, 45, 48–50

VANITY, as theme, 30–31

WARFARE, as subject of satire, 13–14, 21, 22, 42

YAHOOS: as embodiment of the bestial, 33–34, 50–52; Gulliver compared to, 21, 22, 23, 32; Gulliver's disgust toward, 5, 21–23, 32; as "savage old Irish," 51–52; moral lesson presented by, 28–29; as natural men, 6, 21; and their role in the book, 20–23

SANDY SPRINGS

```
Y
823.5      Johnathan Swift's Gulliver's
SWIFT         travels
```

SANDY SPRINGS
ATLANTA-FULTON PUBLIC LIBRARY
R00901 27402
SS   JAN 2000
                                     DEMCO